COPING IN

A Single-Parent

Home

COPING IN

A Single-Parent

Home

Bill R. Wagonseller, Lynne C. Ruegamer

and Marie C. Harrington

THE ROSEN PUBLISHING GROUP, INC./NEW YORK

Published in 1992, 1995 by The Rosen Publishing Group, Inc.
29 East 21st Street, New York, NY 10010

Revised Edition 1995

Wagonseller, Bill R.
    Coping in a single-parent home / Bill R. Wagonseller,
Lynne C. Ruegamer, and Marie C. Harrington.—rev. ed.
        p.   cm.
    Includes bibliographical references and index.
    Summary: Discusses coping with the problems of living in
a single-parent home.
    ISBN 0-8239-1952-8
    1. Children of single parents—United States—Juvenile
literature. [1. Single-parent family. 2. Family problems.
3. Family life.] I. Ruegamer, Lynne C. II. Harrington, Marie.
III. Title.
HQ777.4.W34   1992
306.85′6—dc20
                                                    91-41178
                                                        CIP
                                                         AC

Manufactured in the United States of America

ABOUT THE AUTHORS ◇

Dr. Bill R. Wagonseller is a professor of Special Education at the University of Nevada, Las Vegas. He serves as Director of UNLV's Parent/Family Wellness Center and coordinator of the Emotional Disturbance Teacher Training Program. For the past twenty-five years he has been developing parent training materials, which are currently used in churches, schools, and agencies and by families throughout the world.

Dr. Wagonseller began his professional teaching career in the Wichita public schools as a teacher/administrator of the Lake Afton Boy's Ranch, a detention center for delinquent boys. He has earned numerous awards for teaching excellence, including UNLV's Distinguished Faculty Award in 1982 and Distinguished Teaching Award in 1983 and the Lilly Fong Distinguished Teacher Award in 1986–87. Dr. Wagonseller has also served as a consultant to many school districts and agencies and has received a recognition award from the Las Vegas Chapter of Phi Delta Kappa for leadership in education. He has published numerous professional papers and scholarly articles, is coauthor of *TIP: Teaching Involved Parenting*, *The Art of Parenting*, and *You and Your Child*, and is Program Developer of the Practical Parenting Video series.

Dr. Lynne C. Ruegamer is a professor of Special Education and Chairperson of that department at the University of Nevada, Las Vegas. She has served as Coordinator of the Severe Mental Handicaps program and Generalist (Resource Room) teacher training program at UNLV.

She received her undergraduate degree in Political Science and History from the University of Montana. Graduate work was completed in Special Education, with emphasis on severe/profound handicaps and behavioral interventions. She has taught in institutions and public and private schools and worked as a consultant for school districts and state agencies.

While active in publishing, Dr. Ruegamer has received awards for excellence in teaching and served on numerous boards. Her areas of expertise include content related to "at-risk" children and youth, parent training, and single-parent families. Her two teenage sons provide "on-the-job" training in parenting and help keep materials relevant for today's families.

Marie C. Harrington is an elementary school teacher with the Clark County School District. She has also worked as a consultant for the Parent/Family Wellness Center at the University of Nevada, Las Vegas, researching parent education and facilitating correspondence between the center's director and parent interest groups.

She received her bachelor's degree in Psychology and Diversified Liberal Arts from the University of California, Los Angeles, and completed graduate work for Teacher Certification from UCLA's Teacher Education Lab. She is currently working on a master's degree in Special Education from UNLV. She recently had an article published in the Las Vegas–based *Kidz Magazine*, a parenting publication.

Acknowledgments

It would be impossible to name all the students, parents, and professionals who directly and indirectly contributed to this book. Special credit and thanks should be given to the students and professional staff at Bishop Gorman and Chaparral High Schools and Cannon Junior High School. The students' input concerning problems and suggestions for coping were most valuable.

We give special thanks to our children for inspiring us and sharing their personal insights into parenting.

We would have never completed the book without the editing, typing, and retyping by Joyce Standish and Lynnette Wilfling.

Finally a very special acknowledgment is due to a colleague, Barbara Ludwig, for her research, interviewing of students, and most of all her professional input.

Contents

Introduction

Your life is changing at a dizzying rate. Because of death, divorce, illness, or separation, suddenly you find you are living in a single-parent home. What exactly does this mean? How will your life change? How will you cope with the changes?

Sometimes it can be very hard to grow up in a single-parent home. Even without the trauma that caused the loss of a parent, there are many problems that crop up and cause trouble.

Just a few years ago, a single parent was pitied. Left as the only parent as a result of divorce or death, he or she was assumed to be incapable of raising a child on his or her own. People thought a father alone would never be able to keep control of the household. If the mother was now in charge, it was thought that she couldn't earn enough money to support a family. However, times have changed. More than half of all teenagers live now, have lived, or will live in a single-parent home.

Living in a single-parent family can mean more responsibility, less free time. It may mean less money or a smaller house. You may have to move or switch schools. Making the transition to a new family structure can be difficult.

But have a little patience. Once you have settled into your newly ordered life, you will be able to enjoy life very fully. The hardest part is making the first adjustments and learning how to cope.

CHAPTER 1

Your Changed Family

One of the most difficult lessons for all of us to learn in life is that no one can predict the future, and often the things that happen to us seem unfair. At times we have all asked ourselves, "Why me?" It's important to learn how to cope with changes, even unfair ones, and to go on.

You are not the only young person living in a single-parent home. Statistics tell us that many American households are changing their form, breaking away from the idea that a nuclear family must consist of two parents and children.

There are many ways to help solve the problems that arise when, by whatever means, a family loses a parent.

A few statistics make the trend toward single parenthood pretty clear. Some five years ago it was reported that seventy-three percent of seventeen-year-old black teenagers and thirty-three percent of seventeen-year-old white teenagers spent part of their childhood in a single-parent home. The figures for 1994 are expected to be higher: it is predicted that eighty percent of seventeen-year-old black teenagers, forty-six percent of seventeen-year-old white teenagers, and sixty percent of seventeen-year-old Hispanic teenagers will spend part of their childhood in a one-parent home.

Those percentages are likely to increase. Each year more than one million babies are born to unmarried women. That means that one quarter of all children come into the world with no father in the home. Many of these women choose to marry, but many more remain single, thus adding to the number of single-parent homes.

From these statistics you can see that you are not unique as a young person who lives with only one parent, but only one of millions of teenagers in single-family homes. These families live everywhere—in big cities and small towns, in rural areas and in suburbs, in rich neighborhoods and in ghettos. They are of all kinds of religious and ethnic backgrounds, some with large incomes, some living comfortably, others on welfare or in poverty. Single-parent homes are filled with every kind of person imaginable.

How do homes become single-parent households? The term "single-parent" has come to be associated mostly with divorce, with one parent still living but no longer at home. The seven million such homes account for three quarters of single-parent families in the United States.

A family headed by a single parent can also be the result of many things, such as the death of one parent, a parent's never marrying, a single foster or adoptive parent, parental job requirements, or a parent having health problems. It is important to understand the circumstances of your living situation in order to meet the exciting realities of day-to-day living.

The new single-parent family faces many changes, some good, some bad. These changes come all at once and can be extremely stressful, mostly because you as a teenager have little or no control over the situation. You may, at first, face a shortage of money, moving, changing schools, changes in your parent's personality, and more responsibilities. You may be asked to help solve your parent's personal problems. Most likely you will suddenly be treated like an adult one minute and a child the next. All this can be disturbing and can cause many problems in a single-parent home.

Studies of single-parent families have shown that young people from one-parent homes seem to experience more problems than other teenagers. They have more difficulties in school. Because they are so upset by their changed situation, many of them earn low grades and are often late or truant.

One possible reason for this is that young people in single-parent homes don't know how to deal with their problems. So much change in such a short time can be extremely difficult for a teen to deal with. However, you will come to the point in day-to-day living when you're strong enough to be responsible for your own actions and feelings. It's a tough task, but you will learn to deal with your complex and painful situation and get on with your life.

For some teens the inability to accept the changes in their lives leads to irresponsible behavior. Some teens can't handle the pain of their family situation, and instead of working through that pain they try to drown it in alcohol and drugs. These teens don't understand that when the drugs are gone, the pain is still there. Getting into drugs and dropping out of school are merely escapes, not solutions for their problems.

The task for you is to learn to take control of your emotions and deal with your pain so you can begin feeling good about yourself. Now is the time to accept the responsibility for your own life. You may want to seek help by talking things out with a friend, or a school counselor, who can help you sort out your feelings and emotions.

A NEW WAY OF LIVING

A lot of things change when your family loses a parent. Many things may get harder; however, some things will improve. When communication is good between you and your parent, life can improve dramatically. You will be better informed about what's going on in the family, and you will have more opportunities to voice your thoughts and opinions.

You have to adjust to having only one parent. Ask your parent's opinion on both important and simple matters. Respect your parent's ideas, thoughts, suggestions—they can be very helpful. Roll them around in your head a bit before rejecting them. See how they fit in with your own ideas and feelings. Discuss the differences with your parent. You may discover that it's very easy to talk to your parent about your personal feelings.

Many families today have financial problems. Try not to complain about always being broke. Complaining only makes it more difficult for your parent. If your parent had money to give you, he or she would. Try to help out with the situation by asking your parent if there is anything you can do. Get a part-time job for pocket money, and don't buy things you don't need. If you are obviously trying to help, your parent is sure to appreciate it.

If the change in your family meant that you had to move, you'll have to overcome the problems that arise in the relocation of your home. You're faced with a new neighborhood, all new faces at school—new teachers, new classmates, a different principal—all of these changes are hard to handle. However, it will help if you keep a positive outlook. New people mean new friends. A new neighborhood means new places to explore. Don't think of it as losing your old friends; you will be able to keep in touch with them. Moving doesn't mean being alone; it means meeting new people. Talk to your parent about any problems you may be having. Tell your parent exactly how you feel about the other kids at school, your new teacher, the school in general. If you have some tough problems, maybe your parent can help you find workable solutions.

The major thing for you as a teen is not to lose your personal identity. Your first responsibility is to yourself— to keep your personal identity separate from the problems occurring between the adults in your family setting. Your personal identity includes anything that you feel is a strength or that you do well. It's possible to get swallowed up in the changes and begin to see yourself as the problem. You must never feel that you are baggage for others. A positive outlook on life will give you hope that better days are ahead.

Being suddenly thrust into the role of a single parent can be a really distressing event. Make an effort to understand your parent's mood changes: "Mom's up one day and down the next." Your parent's general attitude about things may change abruptly: "Gosh, Dad always used to look on the bright side of things. Now, he's as grumpy as an old bear and criticizes everyone and everything." "Mom used to be off and running most of the time doing a million things. Now, she sits at home and just watches TV every night." Don't make up your mind that your parent has suddenly become mean-tempered, hateful, or lazy.

Take a good look at all these changes in your parent. Try to see things from your parent's point of view. All of these changes have pushed your parent into a lot of new situations and have forced him or her to take on a lot of extra responsibility. Talk to your parent. Don't be afraid to offer constructive criticism. Discuss how these changes in your parent are really upsetting or disappointing you.

Consider also that the rules may change now that your parent is alone. The rules that worked in the past—ideals, values, lifestyles—are being tested. This can lead to a great deal of frustration for both you and your parent. When you feel such frustration, try to consider it from your parent's point of view as well as your own.

Many teens experience being used by the single parent to "get back at" the other parent. A parent may act out all the anger that arises from being forced into the single-parent role, whether by divorce or separation. You as a teen can be caught up in a no-win situation. You get the punishment from two sides. Once again, don't be afraid to speak up. Tell both your parents not to drag you into their arguments. Get help from friends to work out what to say. See if you can resolve the issue by communicating, talking to one or both of the people you feel are using you. Use all your favorite methods of persuasion. Explain how trapped you feel at being put in the situation. Ask them to solve their problems between themselves. Next time a battle looms, perhaps your parents will see fit to handle it themselves, not place you in a hopeless situation.

Some parents, on the other hand, exclude their children from all knowledge of family problems. They can be overprotective in trying to avoid involving you in family problems. Maybe your single parent doesn't believe you have the experience or background to understand complex matters. You are in the "in-between" years between childhood and adulthood, trying to assume some responsibility without taking the weight of the world on your shoulders. Tell your parent that you want to know what's going on. Often it's worse to hear about problems through rumors and neighbors than it is to hear them straight out.

If your problems are becoming too much to bear, try writing them down. Keeping a journal can help you organize your thoughts, and somehow writing down all your problems and fears seems to put everything in perspective. Later, you can look back at what you wrote and see how you solved your problems.

Whatever you do, *don't give up*. If there's one lesson to be learned from this book, it is not to give up. Keep trying. Life will not always work out the way you want, and sometimes you will be disappointed. But if you give up, you never give yourself the chance to be happy. If you keep trying, one day you will come out on top.

CHAPTER 2

Divorce

One out of every four children under eighteen in America is living or will live in a family that has gone through a divorce. That's 14.8 million people. Sixty-six percent of all single-parent families are created through divorce. Families of divorce are the fastest growing single-parent families in our country.

Take a minute and think about all the people you know who have been affected by divorce. How many of your friends live in single-parent homes? How many family members? The answer may surprise you.

If you're living in a single-parent home, however, the simple fact that you're not the only one probably doesn't make you feel any better about your situation. Divorce and separation result in many emotional and legal issues. Few kids are prepared for divorce when it happens. The shock, fear, feelings of uncertainty and insecurity, and grief over the loss of a parent cause a lot of misery. Kids have talked about these feelings:

- Divorce or separation signals the collapse of the family structure; you feel insecure because the thing you most depended upon is gone.

- Parents going through divorce are involved in their own feelings and frequently are unable to be the kind of parents you are used to.
- Divorce or separation creates conflicts of loyalty in you. You feel torn between your parents and feel guilt for not supporting them.
- When your parents divorce or separate, you begin to feel uncertain about everything else. You become insecure about the future. Being dependent on one parent also causes great anxiety.
- Your parents are probably very angry and resentful. You may find yourself a little afraid of them. Feeling afraid makes you feel more alone.
- The separation from one of your parents is a very difficult thing to deal with. If you are particularly close to that parent, divorce or separation can represent so great a loss that depression is often a natural reaction.

Going through a divorce, as a parent or a child, is highly emotional. Many issues need to be faced by everyone in the family. Talking about them beforehand and while they are happening makes even difficult problems easier to understand and cope with. In divorce, however, that doesn't happen very often; everyone is too upset to talk or to listen. But ignoring problems doesn't make them go away. Chances are that you find yourself in situations you have little or no control over, don't like, and don't know how to change. Although you can't change the past, it might help you to understand what happened, as well as to get control of the future, if you have a better grasp of what is going on around you.

THE LEGAL SIDE

There are two kinds of divorce and separation: those that involve children, and those that don't. When there are no children, adults can divide up their material possessions and go their separate ways. When there are children, however, all kinds of other things have to be decided: with whom they will live, where they will live, who will support them, and more.

Who decides all this? Many of the issues surrounding your life will be decided through the use of the legal system. A divorce or separation usually involves a lawyer, a legal document (a divorce decree) that represents the decision of both your parents, and sometimes a judge and a courtroom.

You, like fifteen-year-old Ria, have probably heard many legal terms tossed around, a sort of "mumbo jumbo." After the divorce Ria and her two brothers lived with their mother. Their dad visited them on weekends. Ria's brothers could not understand this, and when they asked their dad, he replied, "Your mom has custody, and I can only see you on weekends." Ria said her brothers were really upset over this, blamed their mother for not letting them see their dad, and felt sorry for their dad for having been treated so meanly. She said the boys never forgave their mother for making their dad go away. She said that neither parent told them what custody meant or how the divorce occurred. They just knew that their parents got a divorce, Dad moved out, and nobody was happy!

LIFE AFTER DIVORCE

When your parents divorce it is natural that you will have thousands of new feelings. You may feel anger, fear, resentment, insecurity, and disappointment. So may your brothers and sisters. Most likely, so will your parents. A separation or divorce is by no means an easy thing to go through. The family you knew and have grown accustomed to is changed, and it's perfectly normal to have problems adjusting. However, you should deal with these feelings as they come up, or you may never suceed in adjusting to your new surroundings.

The Divorce Decree

The rules for filing for divorce vary from state to state. In some states the parent filing must state why the divorce is necessary; these reasons given are the *grounds* for divorce. Some common grounds are the following:

- Adultery. One parent is having a sexual relationship with another person.
- Cruel and abusive treatment. One parent is abusing the other parent or their children emotionally or physically or both.
- Desertion. One parent leaves the other on purpose.
- Nonsupport. One parent refuses to support the other or the children or both.
- Prison or jail sentence. One parent is sentenced to prison, usually for more than five years.
- No-fault divorce. Neither party is at fault but the marriage is not working; a divorce is best for all members of the family.

The no-fault divorce is becoming common. One good aspect of it is that far less mud-slinging and name-calling are involved than with the other grounds listed.

Legal Orders

Legal orders are ways of dealing with emergencies that may come up before a divorce is final.

- Temporary custody order. One parent is given legal custody of a child until the divorce is final.
- Temporary restraining order. This prevents one parent from interfering with the other parent's safety or freedom. It might be needed to prevent one parent from giving the other a bad time, or to force one parent to leave the home.
- Temporary support order. A judge can require that one of your parents (usually the one that has left home) continues paying for things the family needs before the divorce is complete.
- Temporary vacate order. One of your parents is required to leave the home, usually because the parents are fighting or one parent is becoming physically or emotionally abusive to the other.

In some ways these orders sound more frightening than the divorce itself. It is important to remember that they are legal decisions and *must* be followed. But no lawyer or judge can tell families how they ought to feel. When parents are not getting along, emotions run high. Parents and kids may do or say off-the-wall things. These orders allow for a cooling-off time so that everyone in the family can back off and take a look at the situation more sensibly.

Mark, a fourteen-year-old, remembered hearing the words "temporary restraining order." His mom and dad were arguing about the new TV/stereo system and "who got it." Mark said that after a long time of fighting his dad picked up a book and threw it at his mother. Mark went to his room, but when the police came he heard them talk about the restraining order and made his dad leave the house. From then on Mark's dad couldn't even come on the front lawn. While confused at first, Mark said that at least if his parents fought they had to do it on the phone instead of in the house. He felt better about that.

Custody

Custody means that the court has assigned one of your parents guardianship (protection) of you while you are under the age of eighteen. There are several types of custody agreements:

- Single-parent. One parent takes full responsibility for the child, who lives with that parent all year.
- Joint
  1. Joint legal. Both parents share in making decisions about the child. Usually the child lives most of the time with just one parent.
  2. Joint physical. Both parents share the responsibility for decision-making and for providing a home and caring for the child.
  3. Alternating. The child lives for periods of time first with one parent and then the other. An example is a child who lives with the mother during the school year and the father during the summer.
- Third-party. The court appoints a guardian, usually a relative or friend; this sometimes happens when

neither parent wants or is able to take care of the child.

Ria's parents had joint legal custody. They had decided for the children to live with their mother and for their father to be able to visit them or take them to his home on weekends. Every divorce involves some kind of custody agreement. Knowing what kind of custody your parents were awarded in their divorce decree may help you understand why you live where you do and when and how you see your noncustodial parent. For instance, Ria's brothers might not have been so upset with their mother if they had understood that their dad had agreed to be able to see them only on weekends.

Alimony

Alimony is payment made by one parent to the parent with whom you live the greater part of the year. The money allows your parent to live almost as well as before the separation or divorce. People married for a long time want more alimony than child-support money (which is described in the next section). Alimony amounts are decided at the time of divorce and are paid until the person paying dies or the person receiving the money remarries.

Child Support

Child support is payment made to the parent with whom you live. The money is to help pay for your food, clothing, and medical/educational expenses. Child support is considered as belonging to you and must be used for your needs. The court decides the amount, considering the income of the parent who pays.

If the parent fails to pay (which happens often), that parent can be called into court to explain why and actually sent to jail for continued failure. Child support stops when you reach the age of eighteen.

Most single-parent families have less money after a divorce than before. The lack of money causes hard feelings all around. It is important for you to realize that child support payments are to be used to help your custodial parent with living expenses as well. You may look at the money as a new pair of tennis shoes; your mom may view it as helping pay for your telephone bill or braces.

Your role in the legal issues surrounding a divorce may depend on how much you understand about the family's problems, how much you feel you need to be involved, *and* how your parents feel about your input. Sometimes parents don't want their children involved. They may want to protect you from being hurt, or think they "know better." Many of the things decided in the divorce decree will have quite an effect on your life. If you want to know what is going on, you are probably mature enough to talk to your parents about these legal things. Depending on your age (usually over fourteen), the court may even take your ideas into consideration as long as they are sensible. Your interest and concern may make a difference, but you need to be informed, then deal with them directly.

"Last time my parents fought, it was about who I'd spend the weekend with. Know what? I don't think either one of them wanted me. Why didn't they just say so?"

asked sixteen-year-old Kurt. Kurt was angry, but he was also hurt and insecure. Since he felt all those things and also rejected, he ran out of the house without telling his parents where he was going. He didn't come back until late that night. By then his parents were really concerned for his safety and angry with him for being so inconsiderate, and Kurt didn't feel much better either. When asked how he dealt with facing two angry parents, Kurt said, "I went to bed!" Kurt belongs to a youth support group that deals with issues like this, along with many others. When asked by the group what he thought he could have done better, Kurt said that running away only aggravated the situation and made everyone madder. Kurt *was* hurt, angry, and insecure, but he didn't tell anyone that, including his parents. He later said what he should have done was to tell his parents while they were arguing, "Wait a minute! You guys are making me feel like I'm not wanted—and that really makes me feel lousy!"

The best way to deal with your feelings is to talk about them. Communicate with your parents, your friends, a counselor, a group. Talk to someone who will listen. If nothing else, write them down in a journal or even on a loose sheet of paper. Once you have identified situations that make you feel angry or insecure, you can decide what to do about those situations. You can avoid them, confront and try to stop them, or learn to accept and deal with them. Avoiding a problem is usually not the best solution, but sometimes if you cannot change the situation, avoiding it gives you time to think about it. Do not just sit on your feelings or try to pretend the problems aren't there. They *are* there, and ignoring them doesn't make them go away; it just makes them fester. Do your best to work them out.

There are also bad ways of dealing with your feelings. Even though you know this, sometimes you can't help yourself and just react rather than thinking things out. Kurt did that. Don't take your anger out on other people, or on your grades at school. Play basketball, sit down and draw, write a story, or play a game. Having problems with your parents or family is hard, but you can't let it ruin your life, your fun, and your relationships with them. That only makes things worse.

While you are getting better at dealing with your feelings—you might want to realize that your brothers and sisters, even your parents, are having the same trouble. Lending a helping hand, or ear, can make a big difference in your life as well as theirs. Think about offering to talk or listen the next time someone you care about is stressed out. Sometimes giving help is as important as receiving it.

CHANGES

The people you have been used to in your life will change, just as you will. It may take time to adjust and understand those changes and learn to deal with them.

Brian, a seventeen-year-old, remembered his mother's changing a lot. "She used to be always smiling and joking. She had a lot of friends over on the weekend for coffee and stuff. Now she never does anything and is always grumpy and yelling at me. No matter what I do she gets mad. She acts like it's my fault that Dad left!"

Marlene is ten years old. She always fought with her sister, Ann. Her dad would blow up every night when he came home from work. "I work all day and come home to this! What's the matter with you two? I should have stayed at work; at least I have peace and quiet there."

Many kids don't blame their mother or father for the divorce. They blame themselves. Brian and Marlene have that feeling. Do you blame yourself for your parents' divorce? You may think you did something to make the divorce happen, or you may just feel angry or sad all the time. It is important to remember that your parents' divorce is *not* your fault. A divorce is not between parents and children; it is between husband and wife. In spite of how your parents change, you need to remember that they still love you but are probably angry and hurt at the changes in their life. Sometimes parents, like kids, take those feelings out on people around them. That isn't fair, but it does happen. If you don't understand your parents' behavior or feel that you might be to blame for the divorce, you need to talk to them about it.

Brian said that one day he blew up and said to his mother, "No wonder Dad left! You're always yelling and mean and take everything out on me. Boy, have you changed!" Brian's mom was startled. She had not realized how much her behavior had changed and how bitter she had become. Maybe Brian could have said it a little differently, but the important thing is that he didn't keep his feelings inside but began to talk to his mom about them. When people continue to yell at each other or get mad, it becomes a negative cycle. Someone has to break the cycle and take positive action. It starts with communication, and that "someone" may need to be you.

Before a separation or divorce, your family, relatives, family friends, and your "buddies" have been pretty much the same. This may also change. When your parents divorce, their families and friends may "get into the act." That can cause conflict and more problems for your mother and father and you! Family members have a natural urge to help, which means they may take sides. Family holidays, vacations, even such simple things as telephone calls can become strained, and it may suddenly seem that you have to make choices. Bobby, fifteen, said that one Thanksgiving he and his brother Sam had three places to go: to Dad's, with Mom and her friends, or with Dad's parents. They were told they could "choose" what they wanted to do. They felt really trapped; no matter what decision they made, somebody would get mad. In such situations it is important not to get caught in the middle. Bobby said they called their dad and grandparents, explained the situation, and said they didn't want to make that kind of decision because they wanted to go to all three. Bobby and Sam asked their mom to have the adults work it out and tell them the decision.

It is especially important with close family members, grandparents, aunts, and uncles that you try to help them realize that the divorce has nothing to do with your actions. Sometimes relatives may associate you with the parent they feel is to blame. It's important for you to make them see that you are not either of your parents, and that you are not at fault for the divorce. If you make them realize that you still care about them and want them to care about you, it may clear the air a little. You should be able to love whoever you want without fear of anger, guilt, or rejection. However your relatives may feel about your parent, they have no right to impose their feelings on you.

Often relatives take sides, and speak badly about one of your parents in front of you. This is likely to anger you, and you may want to speak up to defend your parent. It can be good to make sure your relatives know how you feel; however, if they insist on putting your parent down, try to ignore it. They probably haven't dealt with their own feelings, and fighting about it is likely just to anger them more and not resolve anything. Instead of starting an argument, leave the room. After a while they'll get the hint.

One of the hardest things to accept is that sometimes friends of the family feel an urge to take sides. Some of these friends may be closer to your mother, some to your father. When divorce occurs your parents naturally turn to their friends for support. When that happens, these friends may be torn between your parents and feel they have to choose between them. For example, a friend may decide to support your father, which may make your mom feel angry and hurt. Be aware that your parents want and need support from their friends. Expect changes in your parents' circle of friends—changes that could affect you, since you may see more, or less, of people who have become a familiar part of your life. Remember that these people are not deserting you, but are responding to the needs of your parent. You may find it useful to treat these friends of the family in the same manner as your relatives. Explain to them that you are not an extension of either parent. Stress the fact that you are an individual and they should treat you as such. Simple things like being friendly when you see them, remembering birthdays with a card or phone call, and trying to keep in touch will help. However, you will often have to take the first step with relatives and friends, not wait for them to come to you. Extending yourself a little can be well worth the risk of being snubbed.

While we're on the subject of people, it is highly likely that one or both of your parents will start to date.

Sixteen-year-old Mary and her friends were up late one night watching TV when her mom came home with a man. Mary hadn't even known that her mom had had a date. It was pretty clear that both her mom and her date were surprised to find the girls still up. The man tried to be friendly, but Mary said she was embarrassed and angry. She stormed off to her room and slammed the door. She didn't like the man and didn't like the idea of her mom dating or bringing him home to "her" house.

Having your parents date may not be much fun for you. While it's natural for them to move on to new relationships, your feelings about those relationships may vary. Just as your parents are a little hurt or jealous when you spend less time with them than with your friends, you may feel the same way. To feel a bit hurt or jealous is natural, but to nurse that hurt or jealousy until the negative feelings become a part of your life will lead to nothing but unhappiness. Talk to your mom or dad. Don't make excuses for your feelings; just explain them. If you don't talk things over, you may start to take it out on your parent by being rude to these new people who come to your home. That kind of behavior won't make them go away and won't make you feel any better. You can't "get even" with anyone through stupid or rude behavior. Mary's mother continued to see her new boyfriend. Mary continued to be pretty rude, thinking maybe she could drive the man away. One day she and her mom got into a big fight about it. Their conversation went something like this:

MOM: "You don't seem to think I should have any men friends, Mary, and especially date or have them to the house, is that right?"

MARY: "Well, he's a jerk! And it's my house too!"

MOM: "All right, if you want things to be equal, then think about this: You have your friends over to the house all the time. You go to movies with Ron, and he's over on the weekends to study or goof around. Do you want to make a deal? Neither of us will have men or boys in this house? Isn't that fair?"

Mary didn't answer. That wasn't what she had in mind. Her mother went on, "You see, Mary, you need your own friends, male and female. So do I. It certainly doesn't mean that I love you any less, or you me, because we want to do things with our friends, does it?"

You probably see the point. Your parents need their own friends, and they need to spend time with them. At first it may seem that they spend too much time away from you. They need to learn to balance time with friends and with family, just as you do. You don't have to like your parents' friends, but it will make life a lot easier if you understand that they need them. This may sound like a broken record, but keeping your feelings a secret is not the answer to this problem. Talking helps.

Places Change

Will the "places" in your life change? Could be; it depends mostly on the custody decision. You may have two homes from now on (one with Mom, one with Dad), and that could take some getting used to. If your parents' divorce means that you move to another part of town or another city, give your new neighborhood a chance. Take time to get used to the changes. After all, you might even find that you prefer your new situation to your old one. If you are determined not to like it, you won't, and you will make yourself miserable. The odds are that you can't change this decision, so the best thing to do is accept it and make the best of it.

To understand why the places in your life have changed, you need to know some things about your parents' divorce. Often the court has decided where and with whom you will live. The divorce decree may also specify whom you can visit and for how long. In the Andersons' divorce the kids stayed with their mom during the school year but went to another city to spend the summer with their dad. Eleven-year-old Mike's parents switched weekends; he was with his mom two weekends in a row (he also lived with her), and then with his dad for the next two weekends. Knowing this in advance can help you plan ahead. It's also a good idea to be sure that your parents know your plans so they can consider them. Seventeen-year-old Rhisa's dad came to pick her up one Friday afternoon and she didn't want to go. She had been asked to the school prom but hadn't told him about it. Her dad had arranged some fun things for them to do together over the weekend and was pretty mad when he found out about the dance. He felt that Rhisa or her mother should have called him. Was he right to have been angry? What could have prevented this? Everyone is busy and has plans. It is common courtesy to tell your parents about your plans; it gives them time to change their schedules, if possible. After that weekend Rhisa made an agreement with her dad to send him her school schedule and ideas about activities and dates. That worked pretty well; it made Rhisa's life easier, and her dad felt less left out.

There may be times when you don't want to spend a weekend or summer with one of your parents. You want to change the plans. You need to realize that many things in your schedule were decided in the divorce decree. Begging to get your way or throwing a tantrum is not the answer. It only makes things difficult for both your parents and puts a strain on your relationship with them.

You also need to know that the court usually requires that your noncustodial parent get permission from your custodial parent in order to take you out of the state or to a foreign country. Trips of more than thirty days may mean that only one parent gets to see you. The court may not allow that unless both of your parents agree.

Having a court decide what you can and cannot do can be frustrating. If things are really impossible, you might ask your parents to consider your ideas about changes in the custody or visitation and vacation rights. Such changes need to be negotiated. Be reasonable. As mentioned before, courts are usually willing to listen to children over fourteen if their ideas make sense. However, going to court should be a last resort. First try to balance things with your parents.

Situations Change

Did you know that in eleven out of twelve divorces the courts award custody of children to the mother? Statistics indicate that single-parent families have much less money after a divorce or separation. Men still earn more money than women, so a divorce usually means tight finances. Your single parent will have to work, and there is just going to be less money and time to go around.

Try to remember that your parent doesn't like being short of money any more than you do. Realize that when your dad seems grumpy or is getting on your case about everything, it may be because he's worried about the phone bill or why the car isn't working. If there's a shortage of cash for those extras you want, think about how you can earn a bit of money. You don't need to be an older teenager to get a job; there are lots of odd jobs you can do for neighbors and friends. Make a list of things you could do and see if one or two of them would work. Tithea, thirteen, volunteered to sweep the halls and stairways in her apartment complex. She got fifty cents from each of the tenants; that brought in four dollars twice a week. Tithea felt pretty good about having her own spending money. Look around at some of the things that need to be done, and chances are you can do them.

If getting work is not your thing, promise yourself to help out more around the house. Look at it this way: The more you take care of your things, the longer they will last; the longer they last, the less money your parent has to pay to repair or replace them. That leaves more money for everyone, including you. Not too many kids (or adults) like housework or yardwork, but it has to be done—a shared responsibility. If not having enough money is a problem for you and your family, see how you can contribute either through a job or helping at home. You may not always see an increase in your spending money, but you'll probably make your parent a lot happier.

Some parents in this country have been called "Santa

Claus" parents. Their motto is "Spend money, buy love." They load their kids up with things, trying to buy their love and affection. Don't let yourself get caught in this trap. This sort of parent behavior will fill your room with goodies, but will it bring you love and affection? Buying you things cannot make up for the time the parent doesn't spend with you or the visits that are not made. If this is your situation you have to make up your mind whether you want a lot of things or your parent's time and attention. It's not that the "Santa Claus" parent doesn't love you; he or she just doesn't realize that you would trade all the things in a second for a bit of attention. Speak up! Tell your parent how you feel. Explain that goodies can't take a parent's place.

Try not to get caught in the middle of a battle between your parents to be the one to give you the most things. That kind of battle can bring nothing but hard feelings to everyone. Above all, learn to accept both of your parents for who, and what, they are. Whether they give you things, time, money, or love, accept them and value them equally.

Living in a single-parent family, you may find that you have too much or too little of what you want. Either way, as you become older and more independent you'll want to take more responsibility for yourself and work toward the things you want. The earlier you begin doing that, the better you will feel about yourself. It's a great feeling to know that you don't have to rely on everyone else for the things you want. You will have a real opportunity to "take charge" and contribute (through helping out or earning money) to your self-concept, and your family.

Living in a single-parent family that is the result of divorce or separation can be rough at first. It's up to you to keep speaking out so that you can make your life go well for you. If you speak out, the people around you will begin to understand what you need from them. The more you try to work out your problems, and the more you communicate with your parent, the happier you will be. Remember, you cannot change the past, but you can control your own future. You can make your new home life miserable, or you can make it a blast. Keeping cool, talking things out, doing things for yourself instead of relying on or blaming others will take you a lot farther than being bitter or angry. Millions of kids in America share your feelings. They've lived through a divorce; you will too. Take some action, take some time. Things *will* change for the better.

CHAPTER 3

Parenting Without Marriage

I t is often difficult for young people to understand how a mother or father might want to be a parent but not want to be a wife or husband. A lot of personal choice is involved in that kind of decision. Some adults think that choosing single parenting is not the best thing. After all, raising a child is tough; why would anyone want to do it alone? Other people think it's the best thing to do, because they can then devote their full attention and love to their children without being distracted. If you're living in a single-parent home where that decision was made, you probably have your own feelings about it. But the important thing is not to spend time worrying about how you came to be a member of a single-parent family, but rather to take charge of your life.

Growing up in a single-parent family, you will be spared the shock and stress that come from divorce or the death of a parent. You do not have to readjust to a new type of home; your home was always run by one parent. Nevertheless, sometimes it can be difficult to cope with this family structure. It may help to remember that you're not the only teenager living in a single-parent home. The most recent statistics show that nearly three million children under the age of eighteen live in a single-parent home with a parent who was never married. More than two million of these families are headed by single mothers, and single fathers head about 343,000 of them. These statistics show you in vivid terms that there are others like yourself.

What makes some single-parent households different from others is that these parents choose to remain single and to have or adopt a child. Family choices have changed greatly over the years, especially for women. Single motherhood is no longer the taboo it was just forty years ago. As a result, many more mothers are deciding to have children without having a husband. Some of these mothers bear a child; others adopt one. Fathers too are adopting children without choosing to marry.

People decide to be single parents for different reasons. Some want to experience the joy and happy times of having a child in their life and feel they have a lot of love to give. Others believe that they can do more for a child than a foster home or an institution can, so they open their heart and home to a child.

Regardless of the reason for the decision, all of these parents had one thing in common: They were ready to accept the single-parent situation. That doesn't mean that it never had its ups and downs, but at least they were ready to cope without a spouse. Maybe thay had friends to give support when they couldn't handle problems alone; or maybe they had a close family that was always around to pitch in to help. They were able to find ways to hang in there during times when they may have doubted their choice.

Where does that leave you? You didn't choose to have only one parent; you grew up that way. You might find that with adolescence problems crop up in the family that you have never had before. You might begin to wonder unnecessarily if you are abnormal because you have only one parent. You may become insecure about your status. You may be wondering what happened to your other parent, and where he or she is now. If you are adopted, you might wonder who and where your birth parents are.

Part of growing up and part of being a teenager is finding out *who* you are: What are your values? How do you feel about issues in the world? What kind of adult do you want to be? The specific circumstances of why you were born or how your family was formed are not as important as the kind of love and support you received while growing up. In other words, who you are is affected by the things that have happened since you became a part of your family; knowing all the details of what happened to make you a part of your family doesn't change who and what you are.

There are many reasons for a woman to choose being a single parent. Often, a woman chooses to have a child on her own. There are any number of reasons why she may not want to marry the father of her baby. Maybe the two of them were too young to be serious about marriage; maybe he wasn't someone she cared for enough to live with forever; maybe she didn't think he would be a good father. She may have realized that it takes a lot more than having a child together to make a marriage. So she chose to be a mother and not a wife.

Some women plan to have a baby when they reach a certain age. If they haven't found the person they want to marry by that time, they still carry out plans for a child. They are usually in their thirties by the time they start a family and often have a good job or career. Motherhood appeals to them as a way to share their life with someone.

A teenager living in this situation knows one or the other parent well. He or she may know the father but not keep in touch with him or may have no knowledge of the mother. Suppose you're a teenager who lives with your single mother and want to know about your dad: Where could he be? Do I look like him? Does he like the things I do?

Many family experts say that these questions should be answered, but some parents don't handle that well; they may have hard feelings about the other parent that show whenever he is discussed. If you talk to your mom about your dad and she describes him as a loser, remember that she has her own opinion of him. That doesn't mean you have to share the same feelings.

Cheryl is a thirteen-year-old who lives with her mom. When she asked about her dad four years ago, her mom was annoyed and didn't want to talk about him. Cheryl wouldn't give up. She waited for the right chances to ask some questions about her father, like what color his hair was or how tall he was. Eventually the subject was easier for her mom to talk about, and she began to give Cheryl more information. She said that she had been afraid Cheryl would want to find her dad, so she had held back for fear of losing her.

Knowing every little detail about an absent parent is not going to change who *you* are. Asking simple questions first helps to break the ice on the subject. If the parent you live with is not eager to answer questions, give it some time. There may be parts of the past that your mom or dad has not come to grips with. Try to be patient. The answers will come when your parent is ready. In the meantime keep a list of the questions you'd like answered, so when the time comes to talk you'll both be ready.

What happens when a father decides to keep his child? Although it is not a very common situation, some fathers are raising kids without a mother in the picture. These men made their choice to be single fathers for many of the same reasons single moms do. They wanted a child to be a major part of their lives—not an easy decision, but one that shows they did want you.

Teens living with their dad may have a lot of the same questions that Cheryl did. If you live in a single-parent family, you probably want to know about your mom. Again, you have a right to ask, but you may need to wait until the time is right.

Derek, fifteen, had always thought his mother didn't want him. He was happy with his dad and did lots of stuff with his grandparents, but thoughts of his mother's having given him up really bothered him. Finally he discussed it with his dad and learned that his mom had not been ready to settle down with a family when she became pregnant. His dad felt he *was* ready to have a family, so he kept Derek, and he said he had never regretted it for a minute. Knowing that made Derek feel better about being a family of two—just him and his dad.

Another type of never-married, single-parent family comes about through adoption. Statistics show that many more single adults are adopting infants and older children than ever before. Men and women are realizing that they can provide a loving home for a child who otherwise might not have one. Some parents choose to tell their child that he or she is adopted; others choose not to do so.

As an adopted teenager of a single parent, you may feel that you're different from other teens. Yes, you're different, but only in the fact that you don't live with your biological parent. That does not mean that you're some kind of weird person. You are a regular teenager living in a single-parent home. If you have uncomfortable feelings, try talking them out with your brother or sister or your school counselor. Get answers that will take away any doubts you have about being a "different" kind of teen.

You may wonder about your past. One teenager, Ben, wanted to know what his "real" parents were like. He wondered where they lived and why they didn't keep him. Ben got some good information from an article he read in the school library. The article explained that giving birth makes one a biological mother or father. Providing love, security, and the things a child needs makes a mother or father a parent. In other words, anyone can be a biological mother or father, but it takes hard work and lots of it to make a mother or father a parent. After thinking about this, Ben decided that he was living with his "real" parents, even though they had adopted him. It didn't stop him from thinking about his biological mother and father, but it did put things in perspective.

Your adoptive parent, your "real" parent, has probably already talked to you about your adoption. Like Ben, however, as you get older your curiosity gets stronger and you may want more information. That is natural—and certainly something you should discuss with your parent. However, be prepared for it to be a touchy subject. Your parent may feel very insecure and may look at your interest in your biological parent as threatening. Ben broke the ice by giving a copy of the magazine article to his mother and asking her what she thought about it. She told him that when he was born the identity of his biological parents was kept confidential, and the adoption records were sealed. This happens frequently. Biological parents often do not want anyone to know about their having a child. In Ben's case, he can continue to wonder and have questions, but no one can provide the answers for him at this time. To dwell on the subject won't help either. Open communication with his mother provided more information than he had before, but now he needs to get on with other things in his life.

The decision to investigate the identity of your biological parents needs to be made carefully. Your reasons for wanting to know also need to be discussed. Many legal issues are involved, as well as the matter of your family and how they feel about it. Experts tell us that many children idealize their unknown parents, imagining them movie stars, or rich and famous. This is rarely the case. In fact, not knowing is frequently better than finding out.

If your life so far has been spent with one parent, you may wonder how things would be with the other parent. These thoughts come more often when a son lives with his mother or a daughter lives with her father. Sometimes teenage daughters like to talk to their moms and sons to their dads. Daughters feel that Mom will understand better than Dad. Sons think Dad will be more tuned in than Mom. These notions are not always true. Try talking to the parent you live with—whether it's Mom or Dad. If you still feel your parent isn't getting the message, a teenage girl should talk to a sister, an aunt, a grandmother, or a female coach or teacher. In the same way, a teenage boy should try talking to a brother, an uncle, a grandfather, or a coach or teacher. Keep looking for someone you can talk to who can answer your questions.

This person other than your parent can help you sort out things in your life that have been bothering you. Then if you feel stronger about yourself and your everyday life, it may be a good time to bring up the subject at home.

Explain to your parent why you went to someone else for answers, why you didn't feel able to talk it out with your parent. Share some of the things you've learned or have come to understand about yourself and your life at home. This kind of sharing is only fair, and it may lead to a good, rock-solid relationship between the two of you. Perhaps your parent didn't understand how troubled you were, didn't realize how important it was to you to get answers to puzzling questions. If your parent still doesn't care much about talking and sharing thoughts and feelings, at least you've found someone you can rely on in the future to help you over the rough spots in your day-to-day life.

All of us love to tell our own life story from beginning to end. But what might seem to be a missing part—a parent you don't know—may not really be missing at all. Perhaps your story is just different from some of the others. You don't have a chapter on Dad, but you have lots more information on Mom. You didn't grow up with a mom and dad, but you grew up with a parent who cared enough to make you a part of the family. As time goes on, you'll realize that what's important is not what you *don't* have in your life, but what you *do* have.

CHAPTER 4

Desertion

L earning to deal with the absence of a parent is a difficult task in itself. But when one of your parents leaves without forewarning or even good-bye, your whole family may be thrown into a state of confusion. Lots of different feelings come over the spouse and children who are left behind, and finding ways to handle these emotions can make it easier to accept what has happened.

When parents divorce there is usually time to prepare yourself for the day when one of them leaves. You have time to think over how you are going to keep in touch with that parent. But when the end of your parents' marriage is marked by one parent's just running away, you have no chance to prepare—one day the parent is here, the next day, gone. It is scary not knowing where your mom or dad is or whether or not the one who left is ever coming back. Maybe it will help to know something about parents who leave the family. If you know why, the "What am I going to do?" question may be easier to answer.

Researchers have difficulty estimating the number of parents who leave home. Many such parents will do almost anything to keep from being found. If they call to reassure the family, it may be from a number that can't be traced. Being found may mean being forced to face the problems that they ran from in the first place, so they become experts at hiding. Try not to spend time dreaming about how you're going to find your parent. It can be disappointing and a waste of your time and energy.

Many people say that a parent who runs away is morally wrong. After all, everyone has problems, but not everyone quits. If someone does quit by running, he or she must be a weak or a bad person. Don't believe that! Some parents cannot handle all the problems of a family; that doesn't make them weak or bad. It's not fair to describe all of them that way. Try to come up with a fair answer as to why your parent left, one that you can live with without hating your parent.

Rather than *choosing* to run, some people actually *need* to run. They need time away to help them calm down and sort out the confusion in their lives. When they get a grip on things they come back. Of course, some never quite get a grip or finish sorting things out, so they keep running. But again, you should try very hard to understand their feelings.

Kara's father left when she was twelve years old. He called the family from pay phones to "check on them" and promised to come by to see them once he got his act together. But two and a half years later he is still trying to "work things out." Kara has gone from hoping her father will return to feeling angry that he keeps putting the family off. She has gone on with her life and wishes now that he would stop playing games and just admit he's not coming home.

In some families, divorce is not acceptable because of religious beliefs or feelings that it is a cowardly way out of a mess. To leave is an easy way out of the family troubles and the social, emotional, or financial costs of a legal divorce. But the parent who leaves ignores the fact that the family members left behind pay a terrible price for a long time. Running away is selfish when you look at it this way. The one who leaves takes the easy way out and you're left with the tough part—a part you didn't choose.

Some people blame the parent left behind for not having made the spouse happy. Some children even blame themselves or each other for being "bad" and making the parent want to leave. That is simply not true. The troubles and problems are caused by the parents who run away. If they can't find the strength to deal with whatever makes them unhappy and restless, they take off. No one made them go, and no one can solve their problems but themselves.

Jake is a fifteen-year-old whose father left four years ago. On holidays throughout the year he would come home and stay for a few days. Jake and his younger brother and sister used to think that each visit might be that special time Dad would stay for good, but it never happened. Every time he would leave again, the kids would blame each other. But that wasn't right. Jake realizes now that it wasn't their fault; nothing could have made their dad stay unless he wanted to.

Money is always a touchy problem when a parent deserts the family. Parents who leave sometimes withdraw money from bank accounts, either slowly or all at once, after deciding to go. To disappear is an easy way to avoid paying family expenses.

If your family was left with little or no money, you may need to think a little differently about how much you spend. Let's say that your mom left and took half of the family savings with her. Your dad may not want to tell you this because he thinks you will worry. If you believe that is the case, you should talk to your dad and let him know that you can help out in some way. If you talk to him in a grown-up way, he'll probably be relieved that he doesn't have to hide the truth from you any longer. Then perhaps you can decide how best to handle the shortage of money.

Ana was seventeen when her mother left and withdrew all the money from the family's checking account. When Ana found out that her dad was worried about money, she offered to take a lunch to school instead of buying one, and she baby-sat more often on weekends instead of going out. She also started helping with the grocery shopping by cutting coupons and watching the newspaper for sales. Ana's dad appreciated her help and felt good about having a daughter who could handle things so well. Not everyone can do that much, but every little bit helps when your parent has to take on money worries that were not exactly planned.

What can you do to turn the situation of being left behind into one that you can live with? In addition to money issues, there are many emotional issues to face. You may be worried about the parent who left, wondering if something has happened. It's hard to accept that a parent would stay away voluntarily. Some teenagers in such a situation check the newspaper every day for reports of car accidents. They even call hospitals in case their parent has been hurt and has no identification. Eventually this kind of search is given up; anxiety and fear give way to other feelings as time goes on.

You may feel angry at your parent for leaving without even saying good-bye. Some parents who leave tell a friend or two that they are thinking about it, but others don't tell anyone. You should never feel that if you had known you could have stopped it. Remember, your parent left because of personal feelings. You cannot control what is inside of another person no matter how much you care.

Feeling embarrassed about having one of your parents take off is also a normal reaction. How do you explain it to your friends? You may start by saying that your dad took a job out of town or that your mom's visiting a sick relative. Such stories may buy you a little time, but your close friends will catch on after a while. If you have someone you can trust, explain what is happening. It's okay to let others help you get through this; you don't have to deal with it alone. Friends your age may make you feel better, but adults that you feel comfortable with, such as a school counselor or a coach, might be able to give you a different point of view, to help you over some of the rough days.

You cannot deny the fact that your family has been upset and suddenly forced into a difficult situation. You may see changes in the parent who is still at home, changes you don't understand. Sometimes that parent becomes depressed and feels worthless, hurt, and rejected.

Be patient. Your parent's feelings may change over time. As those feelings start to turn to anger, the parent may snap at you or be very short-tempered. Try not to be too upset or angry about it. Talk to your parent about how *you* feel. Your parent may even think that you blame him or her for the other parent's leaving. If your family is to get through this, you need to talk and work together. Throwing blame around only hurts the rest of the family and causes bad feelings. Chapter 7 contains other helpful suggestions that might work in your specific situation.

When one of your parents leaves, you'll have to deal with many different things. It's best if you tackle just one at a time. Write down all the things you'll have to do differently and arrange them in order of importance. If your dad drove you to baseball practice on weekends, but now he's gone, that should go on your list. Take one thing at a time and see what ways you can come up with to solve it. Again, it's okay to ask for help. Friends and family who care about you will do what they can to make all these big changes in your life easier.

It is natural for you to keep thinking that tomorrow your parent will come back for good, but you can't keep on kidding yourself. You have to admit that some parents leave home forever. You really must get on with your own life, accepting the fact that this is how things will be from now on. Yes, it's painful to accept, but necessary if you want to be anywhere near happy again. It won't be easy to go on, but you can find in yourself the strength not to quit.

Often in situations like this the family keeps looking for the parent who has left, but that is pretty much a waste of time. It's better by far just to let go—but for those who cannot do that right away some services that help families in the search are listed at the end of this chapter. For those able to accept their one-parent home life, keep trying to find ways that will make things better for all the family and especially for yourself.

The teen years are tough enough when everything is going smoothly. No one is saying that you can handle everything without ever needing help. But the things that you can do to take charge of some part of your life are there; you just need to find them with a little help. Talk to the parent who is still at home; go to other adults you trust for advice; don't keep away from your friends. No matter how bad things seem, there's always something good to look for. That something may be the fact that you are still working hard to make your life as great as it can be. Don't give up on yourself, because *you* can make a difference in your family's life as well as your own.

STATE CHILD SUPPORT ENFORCEMENT AGENCIES

ALABAMA
Bureau of Child Support
Alabama Department of
    Pensions and Security
50 Ripley Street
Montgomery, AL 36130
(205) 242-9300

ALASKA
Child Support Enforcement
    Division
Department of Revenue
550 West 7th Avenue
Anchorage, AK 99501
(907) 276-3441

ARIZONA
Child Support Enforcement
    Administration
Department of Economic
    Security
P.O. Box 40458—Site Code
    966-C
Phoenix, AZ 85067
(602) 253-5206

ARKANSAS
Division of Child Support
    Enforcement
Arkansas Social Services
P.O. Box 3358
Little Rock, AR 72203
(501) 371-2464

CALIFORNIA
Child Support Program
    Management Branch
Department of Social Services
744 P Street Mail Stop 9-011
Sacramento, CA 95814
(916) 322-8495

COLORADO
Division of Child Support
    Enforcement
Department of Social Services
717 17th Street
P.O. Box 181000
Denver, CO 80218-0899
(303) 294-5994

CONNECTICUT
Bureau of Child Support
    Enforcement
Department of Human
    Resources
1049 Asylum Avenue
Hartford, CT 06105
(203) 566-3053

DELAWARE
Division of Child Support
    Enforcement
Department of Health and
    Social Services
P.O. Box 904
New Castle, DE 19720
(302) 421-8300

DISTRICT OF COLUMBIA
Office of Paternity and Child
  Support
Department of Human Services
425 I Street NW
Washington, DC 20009
(202) 724-5610

FLORIDA
Office of Child Support
  Enforcement
Department of Health and
  Rehab Services
1317 Winewood Boulevard—
  Bldg 3
Tallahassee, FL 32399–0700
(904) 488-9900

GEORGIA
Office of Child Support
  Recovery
State Department of Human
  Resources
P.O. Box 80000
Atlanta, GA 30357
(404) 894-4119

GUAM
Child Support Enforcement
  Office
Dept. of Public Health and
  Social Services
194 Hernan Cortez Avenue
Agana, GU 96910
(671) 477-2036

HAWAII
Child Support Enforcement
  Agency

Department of Attorney
  General
770 Kapiolani Boulevard
Honolulu, HI 96813
(808) 548-5779

IDAHO
Bureau of Child Support
  Enforcement
Department of Health and
  Welfare
Statehouse Mail
Boise, ID 83720
(208) 334-5710

ILLINOIS
Bureau of Child Support
  Enforcement
Illinois Department of Public
  Aid
P.O. Box 2127
100 South Grand Avenue East
Springfield, IL 62705
(217) 782-1366

INDIANA
Child Support Enforcement
  Division
Department of Public Welfare
141 South Meridian Street
Indianapolis, IN 46225
(317) 232-4885

IOWA
Bureau of Collections
Iowa Department of Human
  Services
Hoover Building
Des Moines, IA 50319
(515) 281-5580

KANSAS
Child Support Enforcement
    Program
Dept. of Social and
    Rehabilitation Services
2700 West Sixth
Topeka, KS 66606
(913) 296-3237

KENTUCKY
Division of Child Support
    Enforcement
Department of Social Insurance
Cabinet for Human Resources
275 East Main Street
Frankfort, KY 40621
(502) 564-2285

LOUISIANA
Support Enforcement Services
    Program
Office of Family Security
Department of Health and
    Human Resources
P.O. Box 94065
Baton Rouge, LA 70804
(504) 342-4780

MAINE
Support Enforcement and
    Location Unit
Bureau of Social Welfare
Department of Human Service
State House, Station 11
Augusta, ME 04333
(207) 289-2886

MARYLAND
Child Support Enforcement
    Administration

Department of Human
    Resources
11 East Mount Royal Avenue
Baltimore, MD 21201
(301) 333-3978

MASSACHUSETTS
Department of Revenue
Child Support Enforcement
    Division
215 First Street
Cambridge, MA 02142
(617) 621-4200

MICHIGAN
Office of Child Support
Department of Social Services
300 South Capital Avenue
Lansing, MI 48909
(517) 373-7570

MINNESOTA
Office of Child Support
Department of Human Services
Metro Square Building
St. Paul, MN 55101
(612) 296-2499

MISSISSIPPI
Child Support Division
State Department of Public
    Welfare
P.O. Box 352
515 East Amite Street
Jackson, MS 39205
(601) 354-0341, ext. 503

MISSOURI
Division of Child Support
    Enforcement

Department of Social Services
P.O. Box 1527
Jefferson City, MO 65102-1527
(314) 751-4301

MONTANA
Child Support Enforcement
  Program
Department of Revenue
Investigation and Enforcement
  Division
Helena, MT 59604
(406) 444-4614

NEBRASKA
Child Support Enforcement
  Office
Department of Social Services
P.O. Box 95026
Lincoln, NE 68509
(402) 471-9125

NEVADA
Child Support Enforcement
  Program
Department of Human
  Resources
2527 North Carson Street,
  Capitol Complex
Carson City, NV 89710
(702) 687-4239

NEW HAMPSHIRE
Office of Child Support
  Enforcement Services
Division of Welfare
Health and Welfare Building
Hazen Drive
Concord, NH 03301
(603) 271-4426

NEW JERSEY
Child Support and Paternity
  Unit
Department of Human Services
CN 716
Trenton, NJ 08625
(609) 538-2401

NEW MEXICO
Child Support Enforcement
  Bureau
Department of Human Services
P.O. Box 2348-PERA
Sante Fe, NM 87503
(505) 827-4230

NEW YORK
Office of Child Support
  Enforcement
New York State Dept. of Social
  Services
P.O. Box 14
1 Commerce Plaza
Albany, NY 12260
(518) 474-9081

NORTH CAROLINA
Child Support Enforcement
  Section
Division of Social Services
Department of Human Services
433 North Harrington street
Raleigh, NC 27603-1393
(919) 733-3582

NORTH DAKOTA
Child Support Enforcement
  Agency
North Dakota Dept. of Human
  Services

State Capitol
Bismarck, ND 58505
(701) 224-3582

OHIO
Bureau of Child Support
Ohio Department of Human
  Services
30 East Broad Street
Columbus, OH 43266-0423
(614) 466-3233

OKLAHOMA
Child Support Enforcement
  Unit
Department of Human Services
P.O. Box 25352
Oklahoma City, OK 73125
(405) 424-5871

OREGON
Recovery Services Station
Adult and Family Services
  Division
Department of Human
  Resources
P.O. Box 14506
Salem, OR 97309
(503) 378-5439

PENNSYLVANIA
Bureau of Child Support
  Enforcement
Department of Public Welfare
P.O. Box 8018
Harrisburg, PA 17105
(717) 787-3672

PUERTO RICO
Child Support Enforcement
  Program
Department of Social Services
Call Box 3349
San Juan, PR 00904
(809) 722-4731

RHODE ISLAND
Bureau of Family Support
Department of Human Services
77 Dorrance Street
Providence, RI 02903
(401) 277-2409

SOUTH CAROLINA
Child Support Enforcement
  Division
Department of Social Services
P.O. Box 1520
Columbia, SC 29202-9988
(803) 737-9938

SOUTH DAKOTA
Office of Child Support
  Enforcement
Department of Social Services
700 Governors Drive
Pierre, SD 57501-2291
(605) 773-3641

TENNESSEE
Child Support Services
Department of Human Services
400 Deadrick Street
Nashville, TN 37219
(615)741-1820

TEXAS
Child Support Enforcement
  Division
Office of Attorney General
P.O. Box 12548
Austin, TX 78711-2548
(512) 463-2181

UTAH
Office of Recovery Service
Department of Social Services
120 North 200 West
P.O. Box 45011
Salt Lake City, UT 84145-0011
(801) 538-4402

VERMONT
Child Support Division
Department of Social Welfare
103 South Main Street
Waterbury, VT 05676
(802) 241-2868

VIRGIN ISLANDS
Support and Paternity Division
Department of Law
46 Norre Gade
St. Thomas, VI 00801
(809) 776-0372

VIRGINIA
Division of Support
  Enforcement
Department of Social Services
8004 Franklin Farms Drive
Richmond, VA 23288
(804) 662-9297

WASHINGTON
Revenue Division
Department of Social and
  Health Services
P.O. Box 9162 Mail Stop PI-11
Olympia, WA 98504
(206) 459-6488

WEST VIRGINIA
Office of Child Support
  Enforcement
Department of Human Services
1900 Washington Street, East
Charleston, WV 25305
(304) 348-3780

WISCONSIN
Division of Community Services
Office of Child Support
1 West Wilson Street
P.O. Box 7851
Madison WI 53707-7851
(608) 266-1175

WYOMING
Child Support Enforcement
  Section
Div. of Public Assistance and
  Social Services
State Dept. of Health and Social
  Services
Hathaway Building
Cheyenne, WY 82002
(307) 777-7892

CHAPTER 5

Death

We fear death. We avoid it. To talk about death is not easy; it doesn't seem natural. Death brings with it a sense of "no tomorrow" that is almost impossible to understand. Today one of every twenty children will face the death of a person close to them. That means that in your classroom at school two or three of your classmates will experience or already have experienced the death of someone they love. Like many people, you probably first experienced death through an animal—a pet. Although death is not discussed in the typical home, research tells us that children usually learn more about death through what is not said about it than what is. Robin remembers her pet gerbil. She came home from school one day and it was not in the cage. Her mother said the gerbil had "gone away." Robin was seven and thought that meant it had gotten out and was hiding. She looked all over the apartment but never found it. Several months later her older brother told her it had died. The death of her pet was an "invisible" happening— here today, gone tomorrow. No discussion! Why had it died? What did it look like dead? What did they do with her dead pet?

When Joey's three goldfish died, his dad suggested that they flush them down the toilet. What a silly suggestion about three pets that were part of his son's life! Joey decided to take matters into his own hands. He and his friend carefully wrapped all three goldfish, put them in a shoebox, and buried them in the garden. They even made a cross with popsicle sticks. What is the message here? Both children were involved with their pets in life; why not in death? Both children had come face to face with death, but neither parent used the pets' death as a learning experience for Robin or Joey. Instead, the two kids *experienced* death but really didn't *learn* about death because of their parents' tiptoeing around the "touchy" subject and their own fear of death. From these early experiences Robin and Joey began learning about death. Did either child get enough information to help in understanding death as a natural event? Facing death is something we will all have to do at some time in life, yet our everyday world teaches us little about it. Most of what you know is learned from TV (unnatural death), from remarks your parent has made (natural death), or from talking about it with friends. Somehow you may have gotten the idea that speaking about death is taboo.

What about television? Ninety-eight percent of American households with children own at least one television set. Young children spend over three hours each day (and more on weekends) watching cartoons and TV shows. One source tells us that 70 percent of the leading characters in action programs are involved in violence and death. There are six times as many violent episodes in one hour of children's cartoons as in one hour of adult programs. Television provides a mixed-up view of death. Seldom does anyone die naturally. In fact, in cartoons they rarely die at all! When death occurs it's "in a story," not really happening, unreal—rather like Robin's gerbil, here today, gone tomorrow. Switch on the next TV program. What notion of the nature of death and dying can you learn from such exposure?

American society has changed. Until the 1990s illness and death occurred in the home, an experience shared by all family members. Children took an active part in or at least watched the funeral and the activities afterward. The impact of death was personal. The pain was shared. Death was not an unknown. In contrast, today's society has hospitals, hospices, nursing homes, and funeral homes. All the events associated with the dying and death of our loved ones are removed and distant, a mystery. So we are left with the attitudes and information gained from impersonal sources (TV, books, movies) and the accidental learning that occurs with our families and friends. We know very little about how we feel about death, or how we should feel, or what to do when a loved one dies. This chapter offers some information to help you understand the reactions that people have to the death of a parent or loved one. The information may help you untangle some of your own feelings if you have lost a parent, a relative, or a friend.

Contrary to common belief, people are intensely interested in death. We all share a natural curiosity about the world of people, objects, and happenings. Curiosity leads to questions. Adults may ask questions that are harder to answer, questions that deal with religious or abstract ideas. Children, however, have pretty straightforward questions that need simple, logical, truthful answers. Most of the answers are not frightening. How you feel about the questions and answers will depend to a large degree on how you have been "programmed" (the attitudes you have learned and experiences you have had). Robin and Joey will have very different ideas of death, based on the deaths of their pets. Research tells us that during the first years of life the idea of death begins and goes through stages related to a child's age and the ideas a child thinks. In other words, each stage is like a page in a coloring book: The colors you use on that page depend on how you've been "programmed," but the picture remains the same. Let's look at the different stages in life and how we feel about death as we grow up. We have given you examples of what young people have said at different ages to give you a better idea of kids' views of death.

Stage One: (Infancy to three)
- These children are too young to understand death consciously. They may react to the changes in their lives by crying, throwing tantrums, or by turning inward and not reacting to people. They can become very depressed if they were especially attached to the parent. However, most infants' feelings are centered around their own needs, and if they are helped to feel secure, their emotions may not be very badly affected by the death of a parent.

Stage Two: (Early childhood—four through six)
- Death is not recognized as permanent. It's a "just-for-now" condition that can change. Researchers on death call this condition "reversible": A child knows that a person is no longer around, but this absence can be "reversed"; something has happened but something else will happen to make the person come back to life. Jimmy said the dead

man was killed, but he "had to get up tomorrow."
- Children at this age typically engage in "magical thinking," make-believe, "I can make this happen." After the death of his baby brother, Ronny, five, told his mother, "I'm sorry, I didn't mean to do it." Ronny's brother had a birth defect and died at six months of age.
- Children also fear retaliation or feel guilt over their "bad" behavior that caused the death. Fears of monsters, bogeymen, and magical characters are also common.

Stage Three: (Middle childhood and preadolescence—seven through eleven)
- Death is understood as an irreversible event caused by murder, accident, or catastrophic event (volcano, hurricane, war). These events are external and happen to you.
- Toward the end of this stage, death is viewed as more personal, caused by illness or old age, something that the child could not have stopped from happening.
- Children are really interested in the "gruesome" aspects of death. Kenny wanted to know what would happen if you were buried alive. Greg wanted to know how long it took a body to rot. Other questions: What happens at the undertaker's? Does a dead person's blood turn blue?
- Interest in the mystical, the hereafter, or voodoo aspects of death seems to become greater. June and her friends freaked out over vampire movies and wore crosses for several weeks. Jonathan, nine, lived close to a cemetery and told his friends the "living dead" came out at night.

Stage Four: (Adolescence—eleven through seventeen)

- Death is understood as irreversible and inevitable, something that happens to all of us.
- Death is a reality. A great deal of anxiety about death arises at this time.
- The awareness that death is a reality inevitably results in a kind of distancing that moves it into the future, thus reducing the threat. One teenager said, "I don't think about it much. I'm pretty healthy and have a lot of things to do, so I'll worry about it when I'm older."
- Religious beliefs are frequently relied upon as comfort. Reincarnation, heaven/hell, and life after death are topics of interest.

We have listed the stages to help you think about death in a real way. You may have a younger brother or sister in one of the stages. If a death occurs in your family, you may be able to read about feelings kids have at that stage and help your sibling understand more about it or just about dying in general. Knowing and understanding may help you in a way, too, to understand family members' feelings and, most important, your own. Matthew's younger brother, Rod, had nightmares and had to sleep with the light on after' the death of his grandma. At age five he thought dead people lived in the dark; he remembered the preacher talking about "going forth from the darkness of death into the light." Lana's twin sister Lori became very religious after the death of their mother. Lana couldn't understand it because they had never gone to church. Lori said she got a lot of comfort thinking about her mother being in heaven, at peace and waiting for them.

You may not be able to understand other people's feelings about death. Their coloring book may look quite different from yours, and they may not understand yours. You may not understand your own feelings. Understanding some of these behaviors is a good place to start. In each stage of growing up, a person experiences real emotions, even though they may seem different to you. Matthew thought his brother was acting like a baby, being afraid of the dark. In Rod's mind, his behavior was protecting him from his fears; it was pretty normal behavior for someone his age. Going through the stages we have discussed is a natural part of growing up.

You might find it helpful to examine some of the emotions you felt after the death of your parent or someone you loved. You need to understand what sort of fears, fantasies, and misunderstandings you have collected along the way. Try talking to someone with whom you feel comfortable. Friends might help, but sometimes not; talking about death might make them feel strange and uncomfortable, especially if no one close to them has died. Talking it over with another family member or someone close, like another relative, or even a school counselor, is a good idea. Talking about your feelings helps you to understand and cope with them.

Whenever death is mentioned, you usually hear the word *grief*. Grief describes the feelings and behaviors of people at the death of someone close—friend, parent, or relative. It describes all of a person's reactions to a loss through death.

The reactions to grief begin with the *avoidance phase*. Shock and denial ("I can't believe this is happening") are felt by everyone. At this time the inability to believe what has happened (the denial) is good, because it allows you to absorb the reality of the loss a little at a time, rather than being completely overwhelmed. During this time you may feel confused, dazed, unable to concentrate or make decisions. Gradually things seem to clear up as you begin to accept the reality of a death.

As the reality continues to sink in, the second phase begins, the phase of *confrontation*. Feelings of anger, rage, envy, and resentment ("How could everyone let this happen?") are common as you begin to deal with your loss. Many times anger is directed at other people, frequently without any reason. Bitter feelings may be directed against God, the doctor, or yourself. Knowing that this behavior and these feelings are "not like you" is even more disturbing. Extremes of emotions are felt, and you seem to have no control.

Sonja, a thirteen-year-old, confessed that she hated her best friend for months after her father died. "It just isn't fair that my friend's father is still alive!" Mike found himself crying in the locker room after football practice. His teammates just stared, not knowing what to do. Mike said that all of a sudden it hit him that his granddad wouldn't be coming to any more games, and he just couldn't stop crying although he hated himself for acting like a baby. In this stage it is hard to predict what will set you off or how you will react. These "grief attacks" are scary but gradually go away. They are also natural, a perfect way of healing. Try to go with the flow of these feelings. Just let them happen and don't feel you have to explain them to others. Keeping the feelings bottled up will only make things worse.

A natural response to loss is always thinking about the person who died. You remember what they wore, how they smiled, the things they liked. Monica gathered up all her dead mother's perfume bottles and kept them in her room. Jess kept his dad's baseball caps and never missed a game on TV, especially when one of his dad's favorite teams was playing. He kept the scores and newspaper clippings just as he had done when his dad was alive.

This kind of behavior and collecting things to remind you of the dead person is also a natural way to help you feel less sad. It's a little like hugging someone and holding him close when saying good-bye. As you continue to do things you did before your loved one died, you're helping yourself to accept the death and working toward the day when you can really "let go" of the dead person, really know that he is dead and gone forever from your life.

The last phase of the grieving cycle is the *reestablishment phase*. Your grief gradually goes away and you are better able to cope. The loss is not forgotten, merely put away in a special place where it can be remembered. Now it is time to put your emotional energy into meeting new people, doing new and different things. Doing this marks the beginning of your reentry into the everyday world. Greg was surprised when he suddenly realized he was enjoying the movie he had gone to see with his friends. It was a war story, and he thought, "Dad would have liked this." Somehow, this time the thought did not make him quite so sad. Jess forgot to watch the Wednesday night baseball game; he was outside with his buddies. One reaction here is guilt over not remembering everything about your parent, over having fun, over "getting on with things." Like other feelings and behaviors you have learned to deal with, feelings of guilt are okay, but don't let them hang on forever. Remember, a time comes when you must get on with your own life while still holding fond memories of the person who died.

What are some reactions to others during a period of grieving? After reading thus far and looking back on your own experiences, you can probably figure out a few. Withdrawal is common and is particular painful because it comes at a time when you need all the emotional and social support you can get. The people in your family are going through the same things you are but may be so wrapped up in their own grief that they are unable to help. Many teenagers tell us that their friends cannot understand their feelings, and most don't want to talk about it. Death is scary. Having a friend who has lost a parent or family member reminds them that it could happen to them too. At first they may avoid you or say or do things that make you feel hurt or angry.

Litecia suddenly felt grown up, older, and the things her friends did—like listening to music and talking about guys—seemed pretty babyish. She also felt guilty doing fun things so soon after her grandmother had died. That meant she spent a lot of time by herself, and loneliness made her more depressed.

Randy just didn't want to be around people. He felt restless and didn't know what he wanted to do. "It's as if the death of your parent puts up a barrier between you and other people. You don't know how, or are not willing to try, to get over the loss right now." Being unable or not wanting to get over a death is okay—for a while, but try not to let these moods last too long. Look for help before you lose friends and miss out on lots of good times.

Leading your own life is not always something you can do alone. Often you need other people's help. Give yourself time to heal. The death of a parent or loved one has made you a different person in many ways. You need time to understand your feelings and learn to handle them. Being with people will not be easy, and your social relationships will change. You may feel shy, afraid to love again, angry over your loss, and frightened by all these changes. Above all, try to share your feelings. Help may come from an unexpected source. You may have to look hard to find the person who can really help. Family members are good choices to start with. But, above all, keep looking.

The mind and body work together. When your body is sick, you "feel" sick. Many physical reactions come with emotional reactions to a loss. You may be surprised at how many people have these bodily reactions at the time of or after the death of a loved one:

- Loss of appetite and weight
- Stomach upset
- Inability to sleep
- Crying (often for no reason)
- Tendency to sigh
- Lack of strength and a feeling of exhaustion
- Lack of energy
- Feeling of emptiness and heaviness throughout the body
- Feeling of "something stuck in my throat"
- Heart palpitations, shortness of breath, or both
- Nervousness and tension
- Loss of sexual desire or increased interest in sex
- Restlessness and constant searching for something to do.

All these symptoms tell you that your body is still reacting to your grief. Gradually, as grief disappears and your life begins to be natural once again, these reactions should go away. If they don't, you should see a doctor. But give yourself some time—healing doesn't come overnight.

It should be pretty clear by now that dealing with the death of someone you love is highly traumatic. It requires all your psychological and physical energy to do so in a healthy fashion. All the feelings you experience in the cycle of grief are part of the healing process. They help you accept the reality of the loss, experience the pain, and adjust to a world without the deceased. As you heal, you will be able to withdraw emotional energy in order to invest it in another relationship. In exploring your feelings, you may find that you accomplish quite a lot.

Sometimes you may feel a need for help. Things aren't working. You may see that the behaviors of your other parent or brother or sister aren't "right." It's pretty difficult to decide whether you or a family member needs assistance in working through grief, but some guidelines might help. A single symptom (unless it is very severe) is not significant, but observing a number of the following symptoms may tell you that additional help would be wise (Segal, 1989):

- Anxiety about further loss and preoccupation with dying
- Desire for reunion so strong as to cause a wish to die
- Apathy and depression
- Loss of self-esteem
- Exaggerated clinging to the surviving parent
- Absorption in daydreaming and inability to function in school
- New patterns of hyperactive, aggressive, or destructive behavior
- Stealing or other antisocial behavior that succeeds in gaining attention.

When several of these behaviors form a pattern and persist, they interfere with day-to-day life. Then it is time for help. Your doctor, school counselor, or a family friend may be able to help you find a mental-health professional.

Janie began to follow her mother everywhere. Even though she was only five, this was not usual behavior. One day when she fell and scraped her knee she began screaming that she was going to die, to bleed to death. Another time she fell asleep watching morning cartoons and woke up screaming, "I'm dead, I'm dead." The kindergarten teacher told Janie's mother that Janie couldn't pay attention in school and cried at the drop of a hat. All these behaviors put together were alarming. Janie's father had died about a year earlier, but it was clear she wasn't yet able to deal with his death. They found a school counselor to provide some help.

After Willie's mother died he went to live with his aunt. In seventh grade Willie had gotten mostly Bs and Cs, but this year he was failing most of his subjects. He began swearing and getting in fights at school and seemed not to have any friends. He wouldn't mind his aunt, and he talked back to his teachers. The school principal met with the aunt, Willie, and a school counselor, but Willie didn't like the counselor, so his aunt consulted their preacher. The preacher recognized Willie's need for help and got him involved in a church youth group. The young people played basketball and after the games sat and talked about different things. As the group began to plan a weekend activity, the group leader asked the kids to volunteer their parents. Willie suddenly began to cry. His grief attack came eight long months after his mother's death. He had been unable to work out his feelings of anger and despair; instead, he had gotten stuck in a pattern of bad behavior and didn't know how to break it.

Adults around a child who acts as Willie did need to notice these negative behaviors and do something to help him change them—get to the root of his problem (not being able to accept his mother's death), get him some help (from the church, school, or a psychologist), and offer support to get him back on track in his life.

Living through the death of a parent or a loved one teaches you many things. Most teenagers report that the experience drew their family closer, that they were tougher, better able to handle challenges to come. Being able to look ahead to new friends, activities, and relationships without fear or guilt was a huge accomplishment. Wanting to do so is an even greater one! Members of a support group of students in a high school were asked to suggest some guidelines to help parents deal with death in a family setting. All the teenagers had experienced the death of a parent, a family member, or a close friend. Their advice went something like this:

1. Don't protect us. Let us know what is going on and how you feel. If we can see you cry, we'll feel free to cry ourselves. We need to feel that we belong and to share our feelings with you.

2. Don't make us feel guilty. Help us not to blame ourselves. Sometimes we don't realize that we are not to blame for the death. Adults need to tell us that; then we can deal with it.

3. Let us show grief our *own* way. You may want to cry; I may want to walk on the beach or read a book. Maybe I don't suffer out loud; let that be okay with you.

4. Help us feel secure. Don't force us to make too many changes in our lives. Death has been enough of a change. Familiar things and family customs help us keep in balance.

5. Be there for us. Don't give up on us. Sometimes we don't know why we do things. We're sure to

learn as we grow up, but we need your help with the growing.

6. Let us help each other. Giving something back makes us feel loved and important. Help us to share our help with one another. Help us find out our different needs; that way we can help each other a lot more.

Researchers have developed a list of questions that you and your family can discuss when you are ready to explore your feelings and attitudes about death. Right now your feelings may be too tender. That is okay. Use the questions when you are ready to move forward. Maybe Robin's mother will see the list and realize that through the death of a pet gerbil new understanding about death can begin.

EXPLORING CHILDHOOD EXPERIENCES WITH DEATH

1. How was the subject of death treated in your home when you were a child? What questions did you ask of your parent? What answers did you receive?
2. What most interested or puzzled you about death when you were a young child?
3. Do you remember the death of a pet or other animal at some time in your childhood? What were the circumstances? How did you feel about it? How did other people respond to your feelings?
4. Do you remember the death of a person at some time in your childhood? What were the circumstances? How did you feel about it? How did other people respond to your feelings?

5. Can you identify any ways in which childhood experiences with death may have influenced you to this day?
6. What do you now think is the best thing a parent could say to or do with a child in a death situation, and why?
7. What do you now think is the worst thing a parent could say to or do with a child in a death situation, and why?

Much of life is about beginnings and endings. Everyone knows deep down that death is a part of life, but few will admit this is so. Living our lives is learning what lies between birth and death. If someone close to you has died, do all you can to make your parents talk to you about it, answer your questions, understand your grief, and help you get back to a normal guilt-free, grief-free daily life. You often hear people say, "You know, life goes on." That may sound pretty awful when you're feeling sad about a death, but it is true. Death or not, life does go on for you.

CHAPTER 6

Illness

Throughout this chapter you will find references to "your family." Understand that "family" can refer to any number of combinations: you and your parent; brothers and/or sisters; extended family members such as aunts, uncles, cousins, grandparents. When several people live under the same roof or make a nucleus of loving and caring individuals, you have a "family." So whether it's just you and your mom or dad or any of the above combinations, you do have a "family."

The illness of a parent can be one of the most difficult things to deal with. If one of your parents becomes an invalid and is in the hospital or in a convalescent home, you may find yourself living in a single-parent home even though both your parents are still there for you. It can be confusing, like being caught up in a tornado. It can be either sudden or expected. It will force you to reevaluate both your family situation and your place in it.

When Cindy came home from school one afternoon, her grandparents were waiting. They told her that her father was in the hospital with "heart problems" and her mother was with him. Just the look on their faces scared

Cindy. Even though they said everything was all right, she did not believe them. They looked too scared to be reassuring. Cindy has never forgotten that moment, their faces, or the dramatic changes that took place in her life from that day on. Her father had suffered a stroke, and although Cindy did not know it that afternoon, he would not die. He would be sick for a long, long time—and her life would be changed forever.

Statistics are few on how many families in America have one parent who has a significant health problem. Many diseases (cancer, heart disease, lung disease, diabetes) as well as accidents and injuries can come into your life with an unexpected thud. If you live in such a family, the whole family needs to make some changes to cope with the sick parent. That can be quite a challenge, but one that you may find easier to face if you have some information. You may also find help in learning from other teenagers who have found themselves in the same situation.

STAGES OF FAMILY ILLNESS

Finding Out

Dealing with a family illness goes in stages. The first stage is *finding out*. Sometimes finding out that your parent is sick comes gradually, just sort of creeps up on you. Other times, like Cindy, you find out with no warning. Either way, at first the finding out brings various emotions: shock, fear, helplessness, even anger and guilt. All these feelings are normal and a natural reaction. One thing that happens when you get bad news is that the message just doesn't sink in. Cindy couldn't believe it. She was frightened, and questions ran through her mind:"Why did it happen?" "Will he die?" "Who's going to take care of me?" She was scared and couldn't think straight.

Jerry's dad was in a car accident. Jerry was called out of school and went to the hospital with his mother. Sitting in the waiting room, he felt angry and betrayed. Dad was supposed to buy him a new baseball glove this week, and he needed that glove for the big game. Dad always took care of things like that. Now what? Almost at once Jerry felt guilty for thinking of himself instead of Dad. He couldn't believe this was happening to him. Not Dad!

Everyone reacts differently in shock. You don't know how to react, and most likely the people around you don't either. There is much confusion. It may be helpful to you to know that these feelings, as well as many you can't even describe, are natural and normal reactions to hearing news that is unexpected, upsetting. When kids learn of a parent's illness, a question immediately pops into their mind: "What about me?" You're scared wondering about your future. Deep down you've always been sure that your parents would always be around to take care of you. Even though you know they're not perfect, you still need to know you can count on them to look after everything. It's a shock to come face to face with the fact that maybe you can't count on that anymore. Cindy reacted with fear; Jerry reacted with anger. Most kids say that shortly after learning about a parent's health problem their first thought is: "What's going to happen to me, to us?"

Jerry felt guilty about those feelings, but he shouldn't have. It's natural to want to feel secure. In fact, admitting to yourself that things have changed is healthy. Playing ostrich and keeping your head in the sand won't help you face reality. The very fact that you're worried about your security and future will help you deal with your parent's illness.

At first, everyone around you is trying to figure out what to do and how to act. The people around you change:

Some try to make you feel better but end up making you feel worse. Megan said her relatives kept telling her: "Now dear, keep your chin up," and "You need to be strong for your mother, dear." Megan didn't feel like being strong! Her father had cancer, her younger sister was always crying, her mother was always at the hospital. Megan felt afraid and alone. The more she tried not to cry or get upset, the worse she felt. One day a neighbor came over and asked, "Megan, how're you doing? I'm not doing so well; I think I need a good cry. How about you?" And Megan began to cry. It was such a relief to have someone to share her feelings with and not always have to act strong. She learned a good lesson: Help can come from unexpected sources.

If you feel alone and helpless you may need to take action. The first step in dealing with a parent's health problem is to let people know how you feel. Don't keep your feelings bottled up! Taking this kind of action will let others know that you're trying to deal with your feelings in an honest manner. You need someone to talk to, someone with whom you can be yourself. Like Megan, you may find that person is a relative, teacher, friend, or someone you hadn't even dreamed could help you.

While we're on the subject of feelings, try to remember that everyone is uptight. Some may react by being angry and always grumpy; some may try to keep a stiff upper lip; others may give in to being sad and gloomy. Trying to figure out how anyone else will react can be a poser. One good key is to try to recall how the person reacted in other tough situations. Jeff remembered that his grandma did nothing but clean, wash dishes, and keep busy the last time his grandpa was sick. She didn't cry or seem upset, but she was always busy working and didn't want to talk. Karen's Aunt Babe cried at the drop of a hat and was always upset. Remembering how people have reacted in the past may give you some clues as to the way they act now. But don't spend much time trying to figure that out. Everyone needs to show a lot of patience for one another. Sharing your feelings, either by talking about them or showing them, is a healthy way to feeling better in a not-so-hot situation.

Let's talk about your sick parent. Try to understand how he or she is feeling. And remember always that your parent is the one who is ill. A sick parent can have any or all of these feelings:

- Shock and denial: "I can't believe it! This can't be happening to me!"
- Panic: "I'm going to die for sure!"
- Helplessness: "I can't do a thing for myself!"
- Confusion: "I just don't understand any of this!"
- Inadequacy: "Now I'm good for absolutely nothing!"

Cliff's dad refused to believe that he might lose the use of his leg; he was mean and angry with everyone around him. He kept saying that if he could just get out of the hospital, he could take care of the leg himself. Shock and denial? You bet! Ian's father couldn't stop talking about how he had to get out of the hospital in time to finish a business deal. No one else could do that job. He had to be there! Real panic over not being able to control his activities? Certainly! Marta's stepmother had always been organized and independent. Now she wouldn't make any decision without "checking with the doctor." She couldn't stop talking about her operation and her medications. She needed help in making even the smallest decision. Bria lived with her granddad, who kept mumbling that he felt like a cripple and would never be any good to anyone again. Inadequacy? Yes! If you think about the ways you have seen your parent act, you can probably see that they fit with one of the above reactions or come up with a few of your own.

Your parent needs time to learn to deal with the health problem. Like you, he or she is still "finding out" what has happened and how it will change things. On top of that, your parent feels afraid, alone, and worried. "Why did this happen to me?" "What will become of my family?" He or she is concerned about the health problem and about you.

Sometimes an illness can just plain take over a parent, especially at first. The parent can't cope with the illness and all the feelings that go with it. Fran's mom became so withdrawn that she hardly paid any attention to the kids.

It is to be hoped that the doctors and nurses understand and pay attention to your parent's behavior. At some point, however, you may feel that it is getting out of hand. Just as your parent needs help with the physical symptoms of the illness, he or she may need help dealing with it emotionally. Discuss your concerns with your other parent, a relative, or the doctor. Don't be afraid to ask for help. The doctor, the nurse, or a counselor may also be able to give you advice on how to help your parent—but you need to seek this help. Earlier we discussed how you need to "grow up." One of the ways you can do that is to get hold of your own emotions and try to take charge of your own life and things you can control. Asking for help for your parent may be the first step you need to take.

Getting Ready to Cope

Cindy heard the family doctor talking about her father's stroke. That was confusing because her grandparents kept referring to "it," and her mother called it a "heart problem." Nobody was very specific. Cindy couldn't understand how a heart problem would affect his speech and ability to use his right arm. She went to the library and looked up information on the heart, heart disease, and strokes. She took notes and made copies to take home. She left the copies on the kitchen table, hoping someone would notice them, and her mother did. Cindy told her mother that she was confused, afraid, and needed to know what was happening. Cindy's mother understood then that her daughter needed to be informed and involved, not protected. They studied and discussed the information together.

To get ready to deal with the health problem, you need to begin by getting information. One of the main roadblocks to that may be the people around you. Cindy's mother and her grandparents wanted to protect her by telling her very little about her father's condition. Cindy found that frightening and felt left out. Although you have to deal with the health problem, how much do you want to know? That is a personal decision. Like Cindy, you may be curious and think you'd feel better if you had more information. Megan did not want to know. She found it frightening enough to go to the hospital and needed more time to deal with her father's cancer. Think about it. Illness can be frightening. There are no definite answers. Sometimes there are not even "truthful" answers, because the answers are not known. Megan knew that her father was undergoing chemotherapy. The doctors were not sure it would cure the cancer, but they had to try. Most of us think either doctors or medicine will make us well again; sometimes that is not the case. Doctors and medicine can help but not cure. Knowing as much as you can about your parent's health problem will help you cope, but how much information you want or think you can handle also needs to be considered.

You need information about:

- the disease or injury (exactly what is the problem?)
- the treatment (what kind of treatment(s) is your parent to receive?)
- the medicines your parent is taking (what are they?).

When Dan's father was released from the hospital after back surgery, he had to lie flat on his back in bed for six weeks. He was so often groggy and out-of-it that Dan gradually stopped going into his room. Dan was pretty disgusted by the way his dad looked, and what's more, he had to use a catheter. Dan made jokes about that with his friends to cover up his discomfort. Actually, he thought his dad was worse off than before the operation. One day his dad yelled for Dan to come help him. Dan, although he was sixteen, hid in his room and refused to come out. Later that evening he heard his father crying. Dan was frightened; he had never seen or heard him cry. He heard his father talking: "I hate being like this, like a baby," and "Everyone thinks I'm revolting," and "They're all tired of having a cripple around."

Later that evening Dan phoned his aunt and learned quite a few things. The pain medication made his dad groggy; the colostomy bag with the catheter was necessary because of swelling and muscle paralysis; his dad was becoming severely depressed because of lack of activity and the family's avoidance of him. How come no one had told Dan all this? Why hadn't he asked? It really wasn't anyone's fault, but everyone had to share the blame. Knowing more about the surgery, what would happen during his dad's recuperation, and the effects of his medication would have enabled Dan to understand all the things he found disgusting. Knowing sooner would have made him a little more patient and more willing to help.

Where can you get the information? Make your own list of questions and begin with the doctor's office. Your grandparent or anyone else familiar with your parent's health problem can be of help. Write down the name of the health problem/disease/injury, the name of the medication, and the name/description of the treatment. Knowing what caused the problem may help you understand the treatment. Many medications and treatments may be recommended for one health problem. You will need help in relating all this to your parent's particular case. Remember, every person is different.

Finding out about the treatment and medication will take a little effort. You will learn that there is often a trade-off: Medications to control pain may make the patient groggy and "out of it"; chemotherapy for cancer may make the patient weak and nauseated; surgery may cause a patient to be bedridden for long periods. These "side effects" usually disappear after the treatment and medication are stopped. Knowing what kinds of things will happen as a result of the treatment or medication may help you understand and accept them. You'll also begin to see the relationship between the health problem, the medicine, and the treatment.

A side note: Finding out about your parent's health problem may help you answer other questions that may have been lurking in your mind. Most children are concerned that they may have caused the parent's health problems or will "get" the same disease. You don't have the power to make your parent sick. There are always many reasons for a particular illness, and none is the fault of a child. Phil's father liked to say, "You'll be the death of me yet!" When his dad died of a heart attack, Phil remembered the argument they had had several days earlier. The heart attack was the result of many factors: diet, lack of exercise, smoking, and stress, all of which had been present long before Phil was even on the scene. It is natural to feel a little guilty, but you must use common sense before "blaming" anyone, especially yourself.

Your parent's doctor can talk to you about "getting" the same disease. Some diseases are inherited; others are not. Some diseases may run in families, and relatives may be at risk for developing them. Other types of illness are a result of external events (diet, exercise, habits). By learning more about your parent's illness, you can answer some of these questions for yourself and eliminate a lot of your worry and guilt.

Educating yourself about your parent's health problem is just one more challenge you face. The situation may also bring about changes in your life:

- Economics (less money to spend)
- Social relationships (fewer friends)
- Activities (less time to spend doing things you like to do).

Some health problems last only a short time, even though they can be quite serious. Dan's father was in bed for several months before things gradually improved.

Although "short-term" health problems may involve hospitalization or surgery, they won't last forever. Some health problems last a long time, however, maybe forever. Long-term illness may be far harder to get used to and may bring about far more family changes.

Regardless of the length of the illness, getting sick is an expensive business! Medical insurance may pay part of the bills, but rarely all. Your family will have to plan for the shortage and work together to make ends meet. Earlier we discussed your need to grow up in a hurry, take charge, and learn to handle more and more responsibility. It may be necessary for you to find small ways to save, earn your own money, or help out in other ways. These are not impossible tasks! Some teenagers resent all the money spent on their parent's illness and the lack of money for themselves. Sound like a pretty natural reaction? It is. But having less money may be a fact and will not be remedied by complaining about it. How do you think your ill parent feels? He or she wants to get better but to do that has to have medical help. Most seriously ill people feel constantly stressed and guilty over how much their treatment costs and yet are powerless to do anything about it. You need to think about someone besides yourself. Take charge, help out, save money, earn money, concentrate on the things you can do, and not on things you can't control.

How will your social life change? Mandy had to take over more of the household chores while her mother was in the hospital. Her older brother had to work, and that left her younger brother and sister at home after school and on weekends. Mandy was twelve and more than able to care for them, but her responsibilities left less time for her friends. Maria found herself alone, at loose ends. Her grandmother was always at the hospital with her mother, leaving Maria to take care of herself. Maria was seventeen and often had thought she would give anything to have the house to herself. But now that everyone was gone, she was lonely and afraid.

Not only will your social relationships change, but friends and relatives may play different roles in your life. Family friends may not be around as much since your parent is ill. They may spend more time with your ill parent. Relatives may try to take the place of your parent. Eleanor's Aunt Barbara moved in with them to help out until her mother got home. This "helping out" also turned into a lot of advice and orders. Eleanor didn't like being bossed around. She remembered when her aunt was fun, not always telling her what to do.

There is no way to tell how people will react to your parent's illness. Some jump in and try to help when they are not wanted. Others fear interfering and stay away, when actually you could use some help. Your relatives may ask you to do a lot of things that interfere with your own life and plans. What to do? Well, you can sit back and let things happen to you, or you can try to take charge. Sit down with your family and have a family council. Develop a list of things your family needs, and assign responsibilities. Write them down and post them where they can be seen. If a relative or friend is coming to live with you for a time, get it straight with your family exactly in what capacity. What are the family rules? Who is responsible for enforcing them—Aunt Eleanor or your parent? These are family decisions, and you all need to work together. If the adult in your family has not thought about having a family council, as a teenager you're surely old enough to suggest it.

The kinds of activities you participate in will hinge on your finances and your new responsibilities. Some new activities will creep in, like taking care of your sick parent or visiting the hospital. You'll want to save time for such visits. You may have fewer activities around the house if your parent is recuperating at home. Quiet activities may replace more active ones. Playing cards instead of football may become better recreation for your brothers and sisters. Meal schedules may be changed to meet the needs of your parent. Weekend trips, vacations, and family outings can be changed to include everyone. But your entire life does NOT have to change. You can easily plan more family-type activities so that your parent is not left out. The main goal is to keep some fun in your life, to be creative and do interesting things. Katie learned to play canasta with her grandmother; when her mom felt well enough she would join them. Katie and her grandmother determined to learn one new game each week; this turned out to be more fun than Katie thought. Her mother also looked forward to the games; they eased her boredom and provided a fun way for Katie to be with her.

PARENT CARE

A decision has been made on whether to provide health care for your parent at home or in the hospital.

At Home

If your parent is recuperating at home, you will be involved with the day-to-day care, taking an active part in fixing meals or giving medications. Perhaps someone has come to live with you, an aunt or uncle, a friend or nurse. Your family has decided to handle the medical aspects of your parent's illness at home. Through the family council you have figured out who has what responsibilities. Your home has partially been turned into a minihospital. Many of the things you do have a medical flavor. Meals for your parent are probably planned by the doctor, so your eating habits may change. Family members must know what and how much your parent can eat and drink. Medications have to be given, and you may find yourself helping out or in charge. Some important things you need to know about your parent's medication are the following:

- Name of each medication.
- How long should it be taken? Instructions might read "until gone" or "three times a day for four weeks."
- How should it be taken? On an empty or full stomach? With milk or water? Many factors can affect the performance of a medication.
- What should be avoided while taking this drug? Alcohol, dairy products, antacids, and vitamins may reduce the effectiveness of some drugs or cause adverse reactions. Activities such as driving a car or strenuous exercise may not be recommended.
- What should be done if a dose is missed?
- What side effects are possible? Every drug has side effects; know which ones are good and which ones require a call to the doctor.

Helping with medication is a large responsibility and one you cannot take lightly. If you don't have the above information or don't understand the prescription instructions, talk to the doctor or the pharmacist. *Don't stop asking questions until you understand.* When you do understand, be sure to follow the directions. Everyone knows this, or should, but it must be stated very clearly: *Keep all medications in a safe place*, away from children and, when necessary, from the patient. Keep a list of phone numbers handy: the hospital, the doctor's office, Aunt Babe's. Keeping things organized will help, especially if you're in a hurry or just plain frazzled.

There are other important factors to consider. Your home has been the place where you can be with family and friends. Family rules, customs, activities, and "things" have been familiar. Out of necessity, they may need to be rearranged; even if they don't, you may want to change them. Lisa and Len found that having their ill parent at home resulted in physical and emotional reactions they hadn't expected. During the day, if Lisa's mother could get up she would wander around in her bathrobe. Lisa usually brought friends home after school. Her friends were sympathetic at first but then started making excuses for not coming over. Lisa was embarrassed about her mother's appearance and was secretly sort of glad when they stayed away. Her mother coughed all night, and Lisa felt she could never get any sleep. She became angry at her mother for being ill, resentful that her friends wouldn't come over, and felt guilty for feeling angry and resentful. Sound familiar? It's natural to feel resentment toward someone who has changed your life, especially when you didn't ask for the change or want it. But if the decision has been made and staying at home is best for your parent, make the best of it! All children want their homes to be nice and their parents to be okay with their friends. Being sick is no fun; it's unattractive and usually makes other people uncomfortable. If the way your parent looks or behaves during recuperation bothers you, think up ways to maintain a fairly normal lifestyle and yet not cause embarrassment to yourself or your ill parent.

Len's dad had always shot hoops with the boys. Now, because of multiple sclerosis, he was in a wheelchair and could barely raise his arms. This was not the dad Len knew or his friends could relate to! One of Len's friends came over one day to pick him up for a movie and saw Len's dad in the living room. Dave went directly over to him and said, "Hey, Mr. D! What's happening?" Len's dad said, "As you can see, I'm not playing any basketball, but I'm still Len's dad and your friend! Good to see you!"

Get the point? Illness had certainly changed his physical shell, but underneath he was still the man they had played basketball with. You have shared many good memories with your parent, and more will come. Try not to concentrate on the physical or emotional aspects of the illness that detract from what you have done together. True, Len will never again play basketball with his dad. In the past he had, and loved it, so remember it. Look for new things to share that can be accomplished within the limits of the illness. If having friends see your parent is hurtful, don't do it. Find other ways to stay involved with your friends—and your parent. Realize that during the course of your parent's illness you will feel resentful or angry. Feel it, then let it go. Make positive changes in your home environment, write them down, discuss them with your family, and try them out. What have you got to lose?

Remember to keep your parent involved! Perhaps Len's dad could help him with his math, or they could watch an NBA game together. One family got an idea from a magazine article called, "Notes from the Bedpost." Every night they went to their father's room with a "newspaper" full of schoolwork, newspaper articles, jokes, or pictures they had drawn. During the day they had to let him rest, but this half hour was their time together.

Expect good and bad days. Illness and medication often go in cycles. Your parent may feel better in the morning but terrible at night. Plan your activities around those feelings, if possible. Living with an illness can be stressful. Chapter 7 has information on dealing with stress. You may want to share some of the tips with family members. Offering a listening ear or a friendly smile on a particularly bad day is sure to be appreciated and may help you understand how they're feeling.

In the Hospital

Many people dislike and are uncomfortable in hospitals. Visiting your parent in a hospital and getting used to the environment is a requirement in case of serious illness. You'll need to find out about visiting hours, special rules, and what to expect when you get there.

If you have a strong reaction to visiting your parent in this setting, take it in small steps. Go for a few minutes to drop off a magazine or just to say hello. Work up to longer periods of time as you're able to handle them. Miriam hated hospital visits, but since her aunt worked and couldn't go in the evenings, she visited her mother then. She took things to do and made a list of things to talk about (neighborhood gossip, news, personal activities). Gary could stay only a few minutes with his grandma. All the tubes and IVs made him feel sick. He'd talk to her for a few minutes, then take a walk.

Knowing the kind of medical treatment your parent is undergoing may help you understand his or her appearance or behavior. Chris knew his father's face would be puffed up because of the medication. It was a shock at first but gradually became part of what he expected to see.

When your parent is in the hospital you have to abide by its rules. It may be more convenient for you to stop by after school, but that may be when nurses are giving baths or medication. Becoming familiar with the hospital routine and your parent's activities will help you plan your visiting time. Getting to know the nurses on duty or the doctor is a good idea. A good relationship with them makes everyone feel easier.

Remember that activities are limited. Brent's dad wanted a cigarette and kept asking Brent to smuggle one in for him. Hospitals have no-smoking rules, and Brent knew he couldn't do that. It your parent asks favors and you can do them, that's great. But if the favors are against hospital rules or are forbidden by your parent's medical treatment plan, you can't help. If this becomes a problem, discuss your parent's request with another adult in your family or if necessary with someone at the hospital.

Changes in your parent's condition at the hospital can catch you off guard. If your parent is having a particularly difficult spell, it might be wise to call the hospital in advance. In that way, you can be prepared for any change in treatment, equipment, or your parent's physical appearance or behavior. That nurse you've come to know can be a big help in this instance.

We've spent a lot of time dealing with your parent's illness: tracking down information, learning how to cope with health problems, and discussing ideas to make your parent's care in the hospital or at home a little easier. It's now time to talk about your getting on with life and taking care of your own health.

Now you have a great deal of information and have had some practical experience in dealing with your parent's health problems. You've probably noticed changes in finances, family, friends, activities, and more. One change you may have missed is the change in you! In the midst of all the confusion you probably haven't had time to look back at what you've actually done. Fifteen-year-old Bill summed it up nicely: "When my father went into the hospital I was fourteen. He stayed for six months. It was a really tough time, but my whole family is tougher now too. I iron my own shirts, do my own laundry, change the oil in the car. My little sister can fix a clogged drain. How about that?" You have undoubtedly learned and done more than you ever wanted to or thought possible. Bravo! Pat yourself on the back!

TAKING CARE OF ME

Keeping healthy mentally and physically is a big challenge in everyday life. It is especially important for you. Good health can equip you with enough strength to meet daily challenges. Throughout your parent's illness you have continued to learn new things, make new friends, and have new experiences. But it is important not to let your parent's illness control your life. You are an individual; that has not changed.

An organization called Cancer Care of Cincinnati has drawn up a Bill of Rights for families. Although it deals primarily with cancer, it has applicability for any illness.

- I have the RIGHT to enjoy my own good health without feeling guilty. It's not my fault that some-one I love has cancer.
- Even if only a child, I have a RIGHT to know what's going on in our family. I have a right to be told the truth about cancer in words I can understand.
- I do not always have to agree with someone just because that person has cancer.
- I can get angry at the person without always feeling

guilty, because sickness does not stop someone from being a person.

- I have a RIGHT to feel what I feel—not what someone else says I "should" feel.
- I have a RIGHT to look after my own needs, even if they do not seem as great as the patient's. I am permitted to take "time out" from the cancer without feeling disloyal.
- I have a RIGHT to get outside help for the patient if I can't manage all the responsibilities of home care myself.
- I have the RIGHT to get help for myself, even if others in my family choose not to do so.

Handling the pressure of having an ill parent is a huge task—a task shared by everyone: your brothers and sisters and anyone who cares about your family. Like Bill, you need to take pride in the positive things you have accomplished and move on to doing more. It is easy to get sidetracked with so many things going on in your life. Many of those things may seem negative. Develop a list of goals, things *you* want to accomplish, and continue to work toward them. Write down things that help you handle the pressure: maybe working out when you get mad instead of yelling at someone, or hiding in a corner with a good book or magazine instead of stressing out. Learning how to deal with an illness takes time. You're a teenager, so you have plenty of that! Set goals, try to be positive, and take pride in what you have accomplished.

CHAPTER 7

Coping

Being a teenager is never easy. People either treat you like you're seven or treat you like you're twenty-seven. One minute you are being condescended to, and the next you are given grown-up responsibilities. Adolescence is a rough time, and no matter how good your life is, it can often be hard to handle.

If you live in a single-parent home, your life just becomes that much more confusing. For whatever reason, all of a sudden you find that your life has totally changed. One of your parents is out of the picture, and often the parent you live with will expect you to handle all the responsibilities created by a decision you had no part in making. That can be both flattering and frustrating.

Now that you're living in a single-parent home, your parent is treating you like an adult. You're given both more responsibility and more freedom. If you have younger sisters or brothers, you may find that your parent turns to you for advice on how to deal with them. Because of your age, you are expected to be able to take care of yourself while your parent copes with keeping the family together.

This, of course, further complicates your life. You are suddenly being treated as an adult and you probably didn't realize exactly what that meant before it was thrust upon you. Your parent is no longer taking care of every little thing for you and making sure everything in your life runs smoothly; he or she has other things that must get done. You are now responsible for all kinds of things you took for granted before.

This almost instant change in status can be very confusing. With it come all kinds of feelings that can be very difficult to handle. You are probably still dealing with the loss of your parent; now on top of that you have to do the dishes and perhaps get a part-time job. You may feel angry that you are expected to handle all this responsibility. After all, you aren't legally an adult; why should you have the responsibilities of one? You may also feel helpless and out of control. All of a sudden your world has changed completely, you can't change it back, and you are expected to be able to do all these things you're not quite sure you can do. You may feel lonely, thinking no one understands what you're going through. Your parent is probably extremely busy and does not have as much time for you as usual; your friends may not understand that you can't go to the movies because you can't afford to. If your parent has told you some of the problems and worries that have come up for her or for him, you may find yourself dwelling on them and worrying about what's going to happen next. You may be afraid of the future.

None of these feelings are bad, or weak. They are totally normal and expected. You have just been catapulted into a situation for which you were unprepared. You are not expected to just dust yourself off and go with the flow. However, these feelings are not totally impossible to handle. You just have to think them out and talk them out. Don't deny them; that will only make you miserable. Don't become obsessed with them; they will take over your life if you let them. You have to accept that you have these nasty feelings and learn how to deal with them, so that you can take control of your life.

The first step in dealing with your problems is, simply enough, recognizing that the problems are there. That may sound silly or obvious, but in truth, sometimes it's easier to pretend you have no problems than it is to face up to them and try to solve them. Unfortunately, pretending the problems aren't there doesn't make them go away, and they can get worse and worse while you are ignoring them. You can't solve a problem if you don't admit it exists. No one's life is perfect, and everyone is entitled to a few imperfect emotions. Admitting that doesn't make you a weak or ungrateful person; it shows that you are mature and responsible enough to handle your life.

The next step is defining the problem. You've been feeling unhappy lately. If you don't know what's been causing your unhappiness you can't fix your problem. Sit down and think about where your feelings have been coming from. Talk them out with your parent or with someone you trust; sometimes you are too close to a problem to see it clearly. You might try writing down your feelings if you're not comfortable discussing them with anyone. Sometimes seeing everything on paper can produce startling revelations.

The next step is probably the hardest. Find solutions to the problem. Come up with a workable solution to whatever is bothering you. Once again, sometimes it can help to talk with someone; two heads are better than one, and someone else is likely to think of solutions you would never have considered. Once you have a possible solution, evaluate it; that is, think realistically about whether it can work. Get a good idea about what the results of that solution would be. Let yourself be comfortable with the idea. Then, when you think you're ready, put your idea into practice.

There is one thing you can do that is likely to stop problems before they start. That is to communicate. Talk to your parent, your family, your friends. Communication is one of the ways you can cut disagreement off at the pass. It makes no difference how shy or quiet a person you may be, or how much you hate talking about yourself and your feelings. If you don't learn to talk, discuss, express your ideas, or in other words, communicate, you won't get anywhere in solving your problems. Worse, you will have a great many more problems than you would if you communicated with people.

Not only does communication mean that you have to open your mouth and talk, it also means that you have to listen and understand other people's feelings and ideas. How many fights have you had in your life over a simple misunderstanding? How many arguments in which you were both saying the same thing but were yelling too loud to hear that? If you talk about your feelings calmly, and even more important, listen to other people's feelings, they will most likely return the favor and you will avoid many pointless disagreements. Through good communication you can hear some of your own problems defined, maybe for the first time; often when you hear someone else's words on a subject, the problem takes on a whole new aspect, and suddenly a solution appears. People can help you better if you help them understand your feelings and problems. You owe it to yourself to make your life happier through good communication.

You certainly don't owe yourself a daily diet of feeling miserable.

Here are some tips for good communication:

- Look at the person you're talking with, and make eye contact. This will help him or her realize that you are really interested in that viewpoint, and the person will be more likely to say more to you.
- Listen carefully to what is being said.
- Keep your mind on the conversation. If you let your attention drift, the person you are talking to will assume you don't care about the conversation.
- Speak so that the other person can understand you. Ask if you are making yourself clear. If not, find other words to explain what you have in mind. Otherwise you aren't communicating; you're just repeating yourself endlessly.
- Let the person know you understand what's being said, and that you care. When you nod, smile, or murmur "um hum" every so often, the other person feels you are paying attention. People need encouragement to keep talking.
- Be sure you're calm and have your thoughts together, and that you're really ready to speak. There is an old maxim, "Think before you speak." It can save a lot of misunderstanding and apologizing later on if you choose your words well in the first place.
- Make sure that you and the other person are in the right mood both to talk and listen. If one of you is going to storm away at the least criticism, the effort will be a waste. Pick a time, together, that is good for both of you.
- Have your talk in a place where you won't be

disturbed. There is nothing more frustrating than being interrupted in the middle of a serious conversation just when you're beginning to get somewhere.

• Be patient. Don't let your emotions cause you to say and do things you don't mean, and don't give up if the conversation isn't going the way you want it to within the first thirty seconds. Real understanding always takes time.

These suggestions can be surprisingly hard to follow, but do make the effort. It's worth it.

DEALING WITH STRESS

The odds are that you are very stressed out. You are a teenager, which is stressful enough. You are in a single-parent home, which can be exciting but at the same time is often draining. The stresses of everyday life can cause you to have all kinds of nasty little feelings, which can make you depressed and unhappy. If you don't deal with stress and find ways to relax, you may find yourself angry and sad for reasons you can't even identify. Every time something happens that upsets you, no matter how small it is, if you don't deal with it, you become a little more stressed. Don't allow yourself to become that stressed out. When someone does something that annoys you, tell that person so. Don't be rude about it, but don't ignore it either. Sometimes people don't realize what they are doing.

The more positive you feel and act in your life, the easier it will be to cope with your stress. If you don't let little things bother you, you won't get upset. Stress can have a pretty unbelievable effect on our lives if we let it get out of control. Researchers on stress have found it causes the following reactions or responses:

Physical Responses
Stomach problems
Headaches
Short or rapid breathing
Insomnia or other sleep disorders
Nausea
Diarrhea
Hives/skin rash
Muscle tightness

Emotional Responses
Depression; feeling down in the dumps
Restlessness
Crying for no reason
Moodiness
Unusual behavior patterns
Withdrawal from family and friends
Blaming others
Fear of promising anything to anyone
Feeling uptight in normal situations

Intellectual Responses
Inability to concentrate
Lack of enthusiasm to do things
Lack of interest in details
Preoccupation with negative or angry thoughts
Tendency to make silly errors
Inability to get things done
Forgetfulness
Low grades and loss of friends

Don't be afraid to tell your parent when you're too stressed out to cope with life. Ask for some time away from the house. Maybe you could spend the weekend at a friend's house. Your parent knows what being stressed out is like. He or she knows how hard it can be to cope with things.

Making the change to a single-parent household can be difficult. But once you settle into it, life will improve. The odds are you will have more responsibility and less free time. But you also will be growing up. You will become mature, capable, and strong. And in the end, you will have learned to cope with problems.

Appendix

RESOURCES

Al-Anon/Alateen Family Group Headquarters
P.O. Box 862
Midtown Station
New York, NY 10018
1-800-344-2666

American Cancer Society
1599 Clifton Road NE
Atlanta, GA 30329-4251
1-800-227-2345

American Heart Association
7272 Greenville Avenue
Dallas, TX 75231

Big Brothers/Big Sisters of America
117 South 17th Street
Philadelphia, PA 19103

Cancer Helpbook
1-800-992-2623

Child Help USA
Child Abuse Hotline USA–National
1-800-4-A-CHILD (1-800-422-4453)

Family Service Association of America (FSAA)
44 East 23rd Street
New York, NY 10010
1-212-674-6100

International Youth Council of Parents without Partners
8807 Colesville Road
Silver Spring, Md. 20910
1-301-588-9354

National Hospice Organization
1901 North Moore Street
Arlington, VA 22209

National Mental Health Association
1021 Prince Street
Alexandria, VA 22314

National Multiple Sclerosis Society
733 3rd Avenue
New York, NY 10017-3288

National Youth Crisis Hotline
1-800-662-HELP (1-800-662-4357)

State Child Support Enforcement
List of State Administrators
Deloitte & Touch
3069 Harmony Church Road
Darlington, MD 21034
(410-734-7206)

United States Public Health Service
5600 Fishers Lane
Rockville, MD 20857

For Further Reading

Adams, P., Milner, J., and Schrepf, N. *Fatherless Children.* New York: John Wiley and Sons, Inc., 1984.

Atlas, S.L. *Single Parenting: A Practical Resource Guide.* Englewood Cliffs, NJ: Prentice-Hall, 1981.

Bailey, M. *Single-Parent Families.* New York: Crestwood House, 1989.

Bernstein, J.E. *Books to Help Children Cope with Separation and Loss*, 2d ed. New York: Bowker, 1983.

Cashmore, E. *Having To: The World of One-Parent Families.* London; Boston: Allen & Unwin, 1985.

Dodson, Fitzhugh. *How to Single Parent.* New York: Harper & Row, 1987.

Dolmetsch, Paul, and Jhik, Alexa. *The Kids' Book about Single-Parent Families.* New York: Doubleday, 1985.

Fassler, J. *Helping Children Cope.* New York: The Free Press, 1978.

Gardner, R. *The Boys and Girls Book about One-Parent Families.* New York: G.P. Putnam's Sons, 1978.

Gilbert, S. *How to Live with a Single Parent.* New York: Lothrop, Lee, & Shepard Books, 1982.

Horner, C.T. *The Single Parent Family in Children's Books.* New Jersey: Scarecrow Press, 1978.

Klein, C. *The Single Parent Experience.* New York: Walker, 1973.

Krementz, Jill, *How It Feels When a Parent Dies.* New York: Alfred A. Knopf, 1981.

Ryan, P. *Single Parent Families.* Washington, DC: U.S. Department of Health and Human Services, 1981.

Index